Pichler / Kaufmann (Eds.)

The European Citizens' Initiative – into new democratic territory

Publications of Legal Policy

Publications of the
Austrian Institute
for
European Law and Policy

Edited by Johannes W. Pichler

Volume 30

The European Citizens' Initiative – into new democratic territory

edited

by

Johannes W. Pichler

and

Bruno Kaufmann

BWV • BERLINER WISSENSCHAFTS-VERLAG

intersentia

nwv neuer wissenschaftlicher Verlag

Members of

EAP

European Academic Press

Wien · Graz 2010

Bibliographic information published by the Deutsche Nationalbibliothek

The Deutsche Nationalbibliothek lists this publication in the Deutsche Nationalbibliografie; detailed bibliographic data are available in the Internet at http://dnb.d-nb.de.

Publication in Belgium:
ISBN 978-94-000-0062-9
Intersentia N.V.
Groenstraat 31
B-2640 Mortsel (Antwerpen)
Phone: ++32 3 680 15 50, Fax: ++32 3 658 71 21

Publication in Germany:
ISBN 978-3-8305-1783-2
BWV Berliner Wissenschafts-Verlag
Markgrafenstraße 12-14
D-10117 Berlin
Phone: +49 30 84 17 70-0, Fax: +49 30 84 17 70-21

Publication in Austria:
ISBN 978-3-7083-0647-6
Neuer Wissenschaftlicher Verlag GmbH Nfg KG
Argentinierstraße 42/6, 1040 Wien
Phone: +43 1 535 61 03-24, Fax: +43 1 535 61 03-25
e-mail: office@nwv.at

Geidorfgürtel 20, 8010 Graz
e-mail: office@nwv.at

Internet: www.nwv.at

Print: Alwa & Deil, Wien
e-mail: office@alwa-deil.at

Publications of the Austrian Institute for European Law and Policy

Edited by Johannes W. Pichler

The volumes 1-10 are published at Böhlau-Verlag, Vienna, the volumes 11-20 at Verlag Österreich, Vienna.

From volume 21 onwards the series is published at NWV, Neuer Wissenschaftlicher Verlag, Wien · Graz.

Volume 1: Johannes W. Pichler (ed), Was kann eine wissenschaftliche Rechtspolitik leisten? Symposium anläßlich der Eröffnung des Österreichischen Instituts für Rechtspolitik (15. Juni 1989), 1991.

Volume 2: Johannes W. Pichler/Theo Quené (ed), Sozialpartnerschaft und Rechtspolitik. Veränderungschancen am Hintergrund des Modells des Niederländischen Sozial-Ökonomischen Rates (SER), 1990.

Volume 3: Johannes W. Pichler (ed), Einführung in die Patientenrechtspolitik, 1990.

Volume 4: Johannes W. Pichler, Internationale Entwicklungen in den Patientenrechten, 1992.

Volume 5: Franz Bydlinski/Theo Mayer-Maly/Johannes W. Pichler (ed), Renaissance der Idee der Kodifikation: Das Neue Niederländische Bürgerliche Gesetzbuch 1992, 1991.

Volume 6: Johannes W. Pichler/Karim J. Giese, Rechtsakzeptanz. Eine empirische Untersuchung zur Rechtskultur aus dem Blickwinkel der Ideen, Werte und Gesinnungen. Dargestellt am Beispiel einer österreichischen Demoskopie, 1993 (2 vols).

Volume 7: Johannes W. Pichler, Rechtsentwicklungen zu einer verschuldensunabhängigen Entschädigung im Medizinbereich. Band 1: Die Patientenversicherungsrechte in Schweden, Finnland und Dänemark, 1994.

Volume 8: Maria Rauch-Kallat/Johannes W. Pichler (ed), Entwicklungen in den Rechten der Kinder im Hinblick auf die UN-Konvention über die Rechte des Kindes, 1994.

Volume 9: Johannes W. Pichler (ed), Harmonisierungsbedarf der Jugendschutzgesetzgebung der österreichischen Bundesländer im Vergleich, 1997.

Volume 10: Johannes W. Pichler (ed), Rechtsakzeptanz und Handlungsorientierung, 1998.

Volume 11: Johannes W. Pichler (ed), Die „Neue“ Arbeit. Die rechtspolitischen Herausforderungen, 1999.

Volume 12: Ulrike Aichhorn/Thomas Gamper/Johannes W. Pichler, Jugendförderungsrecht. Ein europäischer Rechtsvergleich, 2000.

Volume 13: Johannes W. Pichler (ed), Rechtliche Strategien zur Bewältigung der Wandlungen im Erwerbsleben, 2000.

Volume 14: Johannes W. Pichler (ed), Pflichtversicherung oder Versicherungspflicht in der Krankenversicherung, 2001.

Volume 15: Johannes W. Pichler, Europäische Rechtsentwicklungen zu Umweltschaden-Direktversicherungen: Die Modelle von Schweden und den Niederlanden, 2001.

Volume 16: Johannes W. Pichler (ed), Embryonalstammzelltherapie versus „alternative“ Stammzelltherapien, 2002.

Volume 17: Johannes W. Pichler (ed), eBusiness versus Recht. Behindert Recht den eMarkt – ohne einem dringenden Schutzbedürfnis zu dienen?, 2002.

Volume 18: Ulrike Aichhorn (ed), Unterhalt – Obsorge – Kinderbetreuungsgeld: aus frauen(rechtlicher) Perspektive. Sammelband zum Salzburger ExpertInnenforum „Frau & Recht“, 2003.

Volume 19: Sascha Ferz/Johannes W. Pichler (ed), Mediation im öffentlichen Bereich, 2003.

Volume 20: Johannes W. Pichler (ed), Rauchen & Recht, 2004.

Volume 21: Christian Spendel, Der Europäische Frächterskandal, Hintergründe und Ursachen, 2004.

Volume 22: Lukas Charisius, Europäisches Gemeinschaftsrecht und Rechtsbewußtsein, 2004.

Volume 23: Konrad Grillberger/Johannes W. Pichler (ed), Selbstbehalte in der gesetzlichen Krankenversicherung aus ökonomischer und rechtlicher Sicht, 2005.

Volume 24: Michael Gruber/Johannes W. Pichler (ed), Wirtschaftsmediation zwischen Theorie und Praxis, 2005.

Volume 25: Verena Stolz, Verbraucherschutzrecht bei Online-Auktionen, 2006.

Volume 26: Johannes W. Pichler (ed), eAuktionsbusiness versus Rechtssicherheit 2007.

Volume 27: Johannes W. Pichler (ed), Verändern wir Europa! Die Europäische Initiative – Art 11(4) EUV (n.F.) / Vertrag von Lissabon 2008.

Volume 28: Johannes W. Pichler (ed), We change Europe! The European Initiative – Art 11.4 TEU (n.v.)/ Treaty of Lisbon, 2008.

Volume 29: Johannes W. Pichler (ed), Direct Democracy in the European Union / Direkte Demokratie in der Europäischen Union, 2009.

Table of Contents

AUSTRIAN INSTITUTE FOR EUROPEAN LAW AND POLICY

Mönchsberg 2a, A-5020 Salzburg,
Tel. +43-662-84 39 80, Fax +43-662-84 39 82
E-Mail: office@legalpolicy.eu
www.legalpolicy.eu

iRi Initiative and Referendum Institute Europe

AGENDA

European Citizens'

Initiative Summit

Towards a resolution on the implementation regulation policy on Art 11.4 TEU nV - ToLisbon

MAY 8TH/9TH 2009

HOUSE FOR EUROPE

MÖNCHSBERG 2

5020 SALZBURG

Dear Fellow-European, let's make the difference!

The European Citizens' Initiative right, to be introduced under Art 11.4 TEU nV, is one of the few key innovations in the new EU treaty. It will play a critical role in bringing European democracy forward in the coming years.

While there is no disagreement on the principal idea – to give half a billion Europeans the same right to launch pan-European lawmaking processes as the European Parliament (EP) and the European Council already enjoy – there is an intense debate on exactly how to do this. A special regulation, a European law, for the implementation of Art 11.4 is about to be agreed.

The EP's committee on constitutional affairs has submitted its recommendations and the EP itself will discuss and vote on these in the near future. Based on their own direct experiences, existing European initiative committees have started to express their preferences on how a European Citizens' Initiative law should be designed and how such a law could contribute to enhancing the legitimacy of the first transnational polity in the world – the European Union.

With the Salzburg Citizens' Initiative summit, the host organizations are now offering a stage for all interested parties to present, discuss and mainstream their views on the options and limits of the future European Citizens' Initiative process. This includes experiences with direct-democratic procedures and practices at the sub-European level, as well as with the more than twenty *de facto* European Citizens' Initiatives launched since 2005, on issues such as energy, transportation, freedom of movement, EU democracy and education.

As the final process of the implementation is about to be begun soon after the 2009 decisions (EP elections in June, Lisbon referendum in October, and the election of a new EU commission) the Salzburg summit will produce a resolution to be addressed to the EU commission and to the council.

This document-in-the-making will address the following questions:

- ***how to get an initiative-friendly climate for useful and constructive transnational participation?***
- ***how to accompany initiatives with supportive structures, so that the initiative instrument becomes not just a vehicle for expressing concerns, but a significant and effective tool for a new system of EU governance?***
- ***how to create appropriate systems of electronic communication between those involved with initiatives, and an efficient system for pan-European electronic signature gathering (e-voting)?***
- ***how to avoid bureaucratic procedures, especially in respect of exaggerated security measures?***
- ***how to establish a European Citizens' Initiative support office or agency?***
- ***and last but not least: how to design a financial support scheme for European Citizens' Initiatives, which satisfies some basic requirements?***

You and your organization are most welcome to join the case for more and better democracy in Europe by becoming a partner in the making of the very first transnational direct-democratic tool ever – the European Citizens' Initiative.

Welcome to Salzburg on Europe day,

Welcome to the European Citizens' Initiative Summit!

AGENDA

Day 1 - Friday, May 8th 2009

Chair: *Bruno Kaufmann* (President, Initiative and Referendum Institute Europe)

11.00 Opening Address

Johannes W. Pichler (Director of the Austrian Institute for European Law and Policy):

Objectives of the conference

11.20 Presentation: Towards the implementation of the European Citizens' Initiative

Bruno Kaufmann

Conference concept – issues and topics

11.40 First discussion, feedback and input round

12.30 Lunch break (reception at the venue)

13.30 Experiences and challenges, barriers and obstacles to validating a European Citizens' Initiative:

Issue targeting, seed fundraising, campaigning, signature gathering, administrative tasks organisational aspects regarding finances, marketing, internet activities, languages draft resolution on the organizational and technical support issues – such as e-campaigning and e-voting and what is to be supported by EU structures the need of a European Citizens' Initiative office – ideas, design issues and location options financial support requirements for ecis from the EU-commission – discussion along the lines of the Pichler/Giese recommendations; other recommendation models are welcome

Remarks by *Michael Efler* (Member of the national board of Mehr Demokratie e.V.) and video messages from across Europe

Conclusion and suggestions

15.30 Global outlook session – the European development as a world- wide trendsetter and its consequences

Remarks by *Lee, Jung-Ok*, Chairperson, Committee for International Cooperation Program Korea Democracy Foundation and Co-Host of the 2nd Global Forum on Direct Democracy

16.00 Coffee break

16.30 Presentation of the summit resolution addressed to the EU-Commission – challenging the EU-Commission to take an active and supportive role

First remarks - panel

Statement A*nne-Marie Sigmund* (former president of the EESC)

Statement *Johannes W. Pichler* (Professor for European legal developments, co-author of the "recommendations" section in Pichler/Giese)

Statement *Karim J. Giese* (Professor for public law, co-author of the "recommendations" section in Pichler/Giese)

Statement *Theo Schiller* (Professor of political science at Marburg University and Chairman IRI Europe)

17.30 Second discussion, feedback and input round

Input by *Phillippe D. Grosjean* (Member of the board of the permanent Forum of European Civil Society)

18. 30 Resumé and challenges for the next day's debates

Day 2 – Saturday May 9th, 2009

Chair: 9.00 - 14.00 *Andreas Gross* (member of the parliamentary assembly of the Council of Europe)

14.00 – 15.00 *Theo Schiller* (Professor of political science at Marburg University)

9.00 **Taking the Initiative, activating the citizens; legal prerequisites for launching a successful campaign**

- discussion on the impacts of Art 11.4 – concept – inspiring or discouraging?
- discussion on the legal impacts of the activation goal
- EU-initiative debate seen in the light of Swiss experience
- discussion on the draft resolution concerning the law-related parts

Remarks by *Tamara Ehs* (Political Scientist, Vienna University)

12.00 **Lunch break**

13.00 **Third discussion, feedback and input round**

14.00 **Summary – results – future cooperation – creating initiative platform(s)**

14.30 **Presenting and adopting the Salzburg Citizens' Initiative Summit Resolution**

14.45 **Concluding statement and outlook**

Theo Schiller

15.30 **Close of the conference**

The European Citizens' Initiative Summit is hosted by

The Austrian Institute for European Law and Policy

Founded in 1989 as an offshoot of an association (NFP), run by the republic of Austria/ministry for science and research and the state of Salzburg.

The Institute's working motto is "law and the weaker party". As a result of that programmatic line the Institute has carried out lots of projects in favour of womens' rights, children's rights, youth supporting laws, workers' rights, patients' rights, rights of the elderly, and pollution laws.

On EU-issues the citizens are seen as a kind of a weaker party. Therefore the Institute's programme for the forthcoming session is about EU citizens' rights. For now, the main focus is on: direct democratic instruments, such as the European Citizens' Initiative and the pan-European EU-referendum, EU citizens' online political participation models and the falling electoral turnout in Europe.

IRI Europe - Europe's global direct democracy think-tank

The Initiative and Referendum Institute Europe (IRI Europe) is a transnational think-tank dedicated to research and education on the procedures and practices of modern direct democracy.

Modern direct democracy facilitates popular sovereignty within the framework of a representative system by giving every citizen the right to initiate new proposals (e.g. new laws or constitutional amendments) and to take part in the final decision-making. As modern direct democracy has become much more common in Europe and worldwide, IRI Europe conducts research activities, offers educational programmes and is involved in analytical and consultancy work.

IRI Europe is a non-partisan, non profit-making association with headquarters in Marburg/Germany and brings together some of the best experts on and practitioners of the initiative and referendum process across Europe and the world. IRI Europe is part of the emerging global network of IRI-think tanks, which also includes the US-based Initiative & Referendum Institute and IRI Asia.

A guide to European Citizens' Initiatives launched

No.	Issue	Goal	Committee	Signature gathering
1	**Oneseat initiative**	To establish Brussels as the only seat for the EP	Mainly MEPs	E-gathering only, without verification email 20 available languages 1,237,144 signatures
2	**Equality for all!**	To extend EU citizenship to all EU residents	Europ. association for the protection of human rights	E-gathering only, with verification email, 22 available languages
3	**Against nuclear energy**	To end the Euratom treaty and to prevent the construction of new nuclear facilities	Friends of the Earth, Global 2000	E-gathering and signature list, 13 available languages 634,686 signatures
4	**European health initiative**	To allow natural remedies Europe-wide and to allow referendums in the EU	Dr. Rath health foundation	Signature list with verification email, 6 available languages
5	**Partnership instead of membership for Turkey**	To prevent Turkey from becoming a full member of the EU	Conservative NGOs	E-gathering and signature lists, without verification email
6	**For a political Europe of freedom, security and justice**	To enforce cooperation on justice within the EU	French politicians	E-gathering only, with verification email, eu 25 nationals only

7	**Efficient 112 all over Europe**	The European commission shall ensure a common emergency service	European emergency number association	E-gathering only, without verification email, 25 available languages,
8	**Help Africa**	To provide an extra 5 bill. Euro a year for people living with aids in africa	Mainly Uk MEPs	E-gathering only, without verification email
9	**Initiative pour un service civil Européen**	To establish a pan-European civil service called "un erasmus de la solidarité"	Mouvement européen-france	E-gathering only, without verification email
10	**Save our social Europe**	Campaign for a social Europe	Volkshilfe Österreich	E-gathering only, 4 languages
11	**1million4disability**	For disabled people's rights, through effective legislation, combating all forms of discrimination and guaranteeing their full inclusion	European disability forum	E-gathering with verification email, and paper gathering, 28 languages, 1,298,365 signatures
12	**Labeling genetic enginered food**	Calling for the labelling of animal products where the animals have been fed with ge (genetically engineered) feed	Greenpeace International	On paper gathering only, ended
13	**Initiatives of applied anthroposophy**	Calling for the support of initiatives for applied anthroposophy	Aktion ELIANT	On paper and e-gathering, with verification email, 11 languages (info), 353,992 signatures

14	**High quality of public services**	To make accessible to all a high quality of public service	European trade union confedera-tion (ETUC)	On paper and e-gathering, with verifica-tion email, in 22 languages
15	**For a European referendum on the EU constitution**	To trigger a consultative popular vote on the new EU constitution	Union of European Federalists (UEF)	E-gathering only, with control and verification mechanism, 13 languages
16	**Initiative for the initiative**	The proposal to implement a citizen-friendly European citizen initiative procedure	Alliance of NGOs and student groups	On paper and e-gathering, with verifica-tion email, in 23 lan-guages, more than 10,000 signatures
17	**Emergency Europetition for Darfur**	Demand to dispatch an international protection force to Darfur	Human rights organisations	On paper and e-gathering, with verifica-tion email (publication and comment option)
18	**Referendum on the next EU treaty**	To trigger a referendum in Europe on Europe	MEPs Diana Wallis and Jens Peter Bonde	Only e-gathering, with verifica-tion email 27 lan-guages, 35,346 signa-tures
19	**Cancer united**	Call for the European institutions and the national governments to act urgently in the interests of cancer patients across Europe	Stakeholders in cancer care, federa-tion of Euro-pean cancer societies	Only e-gathering, confirmation but no verifi-cation email,

20	**European citizenship initiative**	To create a forum on European citizenship for study and hearings with citizens and civil society	European citizen action service	No info on gathering, no confirmation or verification
21	**European referendum initiative**	Campaign for a mandatory referendum right on important changes to the EU treaties	Dr. Rath health foundation	Signature list with verification email, 6 available languages
22	**we-change-europe.eu**	1. Open platform – hosting initiatives, which can not afford a voting tool 2. To trigger a paneuropean referendum for all enlargement 3. To trigger direct election of the EU-president	Europa braucht Initiative, e.V. Association (NFP) Berlin	e-voting only, with verification mail, serving with additional applications, 23 available languages

Bruno KAUFMANN / Johannes W. PICHLER

The European Citizens' Initiative – A New Era of Transnational, Participative Democracy

Coming soon – the regulation of the first, transnational direct democratic procedure in world history: Art 11.4 TEU in the new recently adopted Treaty of Lisbon, which came into force on December 1, 2009.

Two very profound changes have to be acknowledged at this early hour of modern direct democracy on the European level: firstly, the new EU Treaty does define its "Democratic Life" as equally based on indirect and direct citizens' participation. And secondly, the Treaty does install a concrete initial procedure for the direct democratic track – the European Citizens' Initiative.

But now we have to be very attentive and careful, since it has happened many times before within Nation States that profound shifts towards (more) democracy have been undermined by the very (basically undemocratic and citizen-unfriendly) implementation of the principle of people power – making the practical use of the new tools an impossibility.

Hence, now, even before we, the citizens of Europe, would be empowered to launch our first European Citizens' Initiatives, it is time to act, time to participate and time to offer our expertise on the use of citizens' initiatives at all levels. This book constitutes one more building block since it documents the contributions and findings of the 2009 Citizens' Initiative Summit in Salzburg where experts and activists from across the world gathered to assess the cornerstones for the implementation of the forthcoming European Citizens' Initiative.

While the Salzburg Manifesto for the European Citizens' Initiative did take account of the relevant resolution by the European Parliament on the new transnational and direct democratic procedure, the Lisbon Treaty still needed to be put into force. This has now taken place, the end of 2009. As a direct consequence, the European Commission could publish its ideas and questions for the European Citizens' Initiative in early 2010 by inviting all concerned parties to take part in a so-called "consultation process".

The editors and authors of this book as well as the participants of the 2009 Citizens' Initiative Summit highly appreciate the concern and care of the outgoing Commission and especially Vice-President Margot Wallström in not losing time in making the very first direct-democratic tool beyond national borders a reality during 2010. However, there are still many hurdles to overcome before we all can start to file and qualify as transnational citizens' initiatives in Europe.

In the Green Paper on the European Citizens' Initiative presented by V-P Wallström on November 11, the Commission does outline ten areas of concern for the future success of the new tool. These areas include among others the "minimum of Member States" from which signatures must come, the "form and wording of a citizens' initiative" as well as the issue of parallel initiatives "on the same issue". Importantly, the Green Paper also address the "requirement for the collection and verification" of signatures and the process of "examination" of qualified initiatives by the Commission.

All these issues will be important features indeed for the forthcoming establishment of a proper regulation. In our view, especially the issue of the collection and verification will require both innovative thoughts as well as new forms. For example, e-collection of signature gatherings will have to be considered and rendered signatures will have to be checked against pan-European voter lists not yet in existence. In this respect, it will be very important to understand the role of the Member States in the making of European Citizens' Initiative. Since the new instrument is designed to create a direct channel between EU citizens and the EU Commission, both the roles of Member States and the EU parliament shall be very modest. Do not forget that the European Citizens' Initiative is establishing the same right for EU citizens to propose new EU legislation as the Member States (in the Council) and the EU Parliament already have.

So, what we probably will see in the next month is that Member States and the European Parliament will start to understand that the EU citizens are indeed beginning to get their own, emancipated role in agenda-setting – and hence may try to limit or undermine this new track – which of course would be most unfortunate. Therefore, it is not the time to celebrate the establishment of the first transnational direct-democratic just yet, it is time once again to act and work for this right, which above all will contribute to develop a European citizens' identity and contribute to make the EU a little bit more democratic.

To facilitate the most crucial dialogue between citizens and the EU, two institutes which have both dedicated their work to the transnational direct democracy issue, have joined forces to establish the European Citizens' Initiative Summit process, a meeting place and network of experts and activists alike.

The Austrian Institute for European Law and Policy (www.legalpolicy.eu), founded in 1989 as an offshoot of an association (NFP) administered by the Republic of Austria/Ministry for Science and Research and the State of Salzburg, has been in operation ever since according to the motto: "Law and the Weaker Party". As a result of that mission statement, the Institute has carried out numerous projects in favour of Women's Rights, Children's Rights, Youth Supporting Laws, Workers' Rights, Patients' Rights, Rights of the Elderly and Pollution Laws.

On EU issues, the citizens are seen as a kind of weaker party. Therefore the Institute's programme is concerned with EU Citizens' Rights. At present, the main focus is on direct democratic instruments, such as the European Citizens' Initiative and the pan-European EU Referendum, on EU citizens' online political participation models and the falling electoral turnout in Europe.

The Initiative and Referendum Institute Europe (IRI Europe) is Europe's Global Direct Democracy Think Tank, a transnational think-tank dedicated to research and education on the procedures and practices of modern direct democracy. Modern direct democracy facilitates popular sovereignty within the framework of a representative system by giving every citizen the right to initiate new proposals (e.g. new laws or constitutional amendments) and to take part in the final decision-making. As modern direct democracy has become much more common in Europe and worldwide, IRI Europe conducts research activities, offers educational programmes and is involved in analytical and consultancy work. IRI Europe is a non-partisan, non-profit-making association with headquarters in Marburg/Germany and brings together some of the best experts on and practitioners of the initiative and referendum process across Europe and the world. IRI Europe is part of the emerging global network of IRI-think tanks which also includes the US-based Initiative & Referendum Institute and IRI Asia. (www.iri-europe.org)

These two institutes have – without any preoccupied approach – invited the existing European initiatives to address their knowledge, their concerns and their ambitions – on a host of key questions:

- How to create an initiative-friendly climate for useful and constructive transnational participation?
- How to accompany initiatives with supportive structures so that the initiative instrument becomes not just a vehicle for expressing concerns, but a significant and effective tool for a new system of EU governance?
- How to design appropriate systems of electronic communication between those involved with initiatives, and an efficient system for pan-European electronic signature gathering (eVoting)?

- How to avoid bureaucratic procedures, especially in respect to exaggerated security measures?
- How to establish a European Citizens' Initiative support office or agency?
- And last but not least: How to draw up a financial support scheme for European Citizens' Initiatives which satisfies some basic requirements?

The 2009 Summit offered many answers to these questions including, that

- the European Citizens' Initiative Right which is to be introduced under Art 11.4 TEUnv is one of the few key innovations in the new EU Treaty. It will play a critical role in bringing European democracy forward in the coming years.
- although there is no disagreement on the principal idea – to give half a billion Europeans the same right to launch pan-European lawmaking processes as the European Parliament (EP) and the European Council already enjoy – there is an intense debate on exactly HOW to do this. A special regulation, a European law, for the implementation of Art 11.4 is about to be agreed on.
- the EP's Committee on Constitutional Affairs has submitted its recommendations and the EP itself will discuss and vote further on these in the near future. Based on their own direct experiences, existing European Initiative Committees have started to express their preferences on how a European Citizens' Initiative Law should be designed and how such a law could contribute to enhancing the legitimacy of the first transnational polity in the world – the European Union.
- with the 2009 Citizens' Initiative Summit in Salzburg, the host organizations are now offering a stage for all interested parties to present, discuss and mainstream their views on the options and limitations of the future European Citizens' Initiative process.
- this includes experiences with direct-democratic procedures and practices at the sub-European level, as well as with the more than twenty de facto European Citizens' Initiatives launched since 2005 on issues such as energy, transportation, freedom of movement, EU democracy and education.

The essence of all this has been condensed in the attached "Salzburg Manifesto". It is not necessary to outline this here again; it is a very compact and easily understood document. We hope that the real concerns and challenges are clearly aired. A European Citizens Initiatives' Office has been founded, located in the Austrian Institute for European Law and Policy. This is only a first, small step. Next steps are in process.

Salzburg/Marburg, December 2009

Johannes W. PICHLER

The European Initiative – Soon Law in Action?

An Introduction

I. A long short story

For more than a decade, the EU and its representatives say they are willing, or even eager, to give us European citizens a voice. Time after time, in speeches given by high-ranking EU politicians, they have invited us citizens to participate. This was a result of the urgent recommendation in the Adonnino report. In 1995, after the so-called Westendorp report, it was the German Chancellor Kohl and the French President Mitterand calling for a Union of Citizens. In 1996, it was the Austrian Foreign Affairs Minister Schüssel who brought up the issue of direct democracy as a citizens' participation model in the EU.

Some, then, have dreamt of a pan-European Referendum Right. What is this right? Some contented themselves with a petition right to be addressed to the EU Parliament. We have had the latter instrument for years – and let me report it as a stillborn law. And the first one, the pan-European referendum, got crushed in the mills of the Constitutional Convention.

What we finally achieved was the European Citizens' Initiative Right. The ECI is constitutionalized and enshrined under Article 11.4 TEU nv in the Treaty of Lisbon. Not that much, but it's not nothing, either. As a legal historian, I would like to tell you that all development began and still begins this way.

So this is where we are. But the ECI's fate is still at risk if we do not act as watchdogs. We need to put pressure on the authorities to focus on our primary goal which is to bring this instrument to life. This indicates that the initiatives and all supporting contributors need to be very organized.

Believe me, this is a great moment for us today as organizers. We are all committed to bringing forth a pro-initiative movement.

The Initiative and Referendum Institute is well known as a guardian angel of direct democracy development – for many years now. Thank you, IRI people, Mr. Bruno Kaufmann and Mr. Schiller along with Jo Leinen, Alain Lamassoure, Carsten Berg, Jürgen Meyer and many, many others, for how you insisted that the Initiative Right be included in the Treaty of Lisbon, finally. I think all of us are waiting for the day when the new Treaty on the European Union comes into force. Once again, thank you, IRI.

My Institute, the Austrian Institute for European Law & Policy, has done research on Art 11.4's reality and its future. In doing so, we were inclined to side with the issue itself and we resolved to function as a consulting, emotionally subsidizing, intellectually supportive entity for all European initiatives. I, personally, have a second identity. I am running an initiative platform in action, www.we-change-europe.eu, – and this is what I must get back to soon, because one can't do both at the same moment, academic and political, simultaneously.

As a part of the science and research community, we are nevertheless bound to act impartially and objectively. And we have to work in equidistance to the specific initiatives themselves, because, do not forget, within the nature of initiatives is a tendency to be in conflict with each other. Thus, the Institute sees itself as a mediator, even a bridge builder to the authorities in Brussels.

II. We have it now, our Art 11.4. Do we?

Does this imply that we have reached our goal for a new era of direct democracy in Europe then, once and for all? I am still a bit skeptical. To have a law in the books is only to have won the first battle. It's not enough anymore. What we really need now is a law in action. What a working law in action looks like is our topic for today and tomorrow. The Summit must find a brilliant model or at least the "blueprint" for such a model that really works.

So, what are the key challenges? What is our key task?

Well, firstly, in my humble opinion, the most important initial task is to formulate an inquiry, a concept that "guides" the EU officials to come alongside – with a kind of oath of disclosure. We should not hesitate to invite the Commission expressly and urgently to give European citizens an answer on their view of the Initiative Right. We should design a public list of these statements and reactions on our websites. We should invite every key decision maker to post his or her statement of reaction on this list of statements. In case they post rejection, at least this was a conclusive answer.

Secondly: Our key challenges are to make EU authorities listen and to entice them towards a pro-active attitude. We must make them aware of what initiatives really need and what is counterproductive. Who else, if not we, should be entitled to call for an initiative-friendly climate? Who else, if not we, should be better equipped to show the High Authorities what's really there in the European citizens' reality? We have tried on the streets and on the web to involve Europeans with their Europe. We have had to suffer from their European ambiguity, from their European alienation, from their passivity. Thus we are the right partner to let Brussels know what is needed: to give the Europeans a wakeup call from the bottom up. Initiatives have worked hard to get through with single initiatives. Some did so very successful, actually just two, some did with some success, let's say a little handful, some have clearly failed, and this is the majority. But they do have one thing in common: experience.

Therefore, initiatives are the ones who know best what initiatives do and do not need:

- Initiatives do not need bureaucratic procedures. Instead, they need support. Frankly spoken, initiatives need public financial support, in order to also keep them free from back office influences.
- Commission, listen! Initiatives do not need tricky interpretations. Like the one that initiatives should not be allowed to raise constitutional issues. No, initiatives need a positive attitude; they need to be appreciated as welcome assistance in promoting Europe and democracy.
- Initiatives do not need endless requirements. Parliament, can you hear me? Initiatives need supportive and consulting institutions which means an independent support agency to save them from frustration and meandering efforts.
- Initiatives do not need national authorities screening each individual voter. National authorities should support with random control – and nothing more. What are we talking about actually? We are talking about an indirect agenda-setting initiative model that insists (or fails to insist) on further steps by the EU Commission. Okay? So, what we need are easy-to-handle, viable transnational, pan-European e-structures – free of charge, of course – for an e-communication tool in order to advertise, campaign and for successful online gathering of signatures. All we must be able to hinder is the mass attack by hackers. A single falsifier should not be the subject matter of pompous provisions.

We intend to deliver all these and similar advisories to the "legislators" in Brussels.

III. Now it is time for me to take the consequence of the aforementioned double function.

This means that I have to decide now whether I would like to act as an academic or as an initiative representative. I am committed.

Bruno, here is my decision. The chairs is yours and not mine any longer. Ladies and gentlemen, let's take the responsibility to contribute to a better democratic future for our Europe.

Remember: yes, we – Europeans – can! ☺

Bruno KAUFMANN

The "new" participative paradigm. How the European Citizens' Initiative can become the standard bearer of 21th century super-democracy

We have gone a long way. Some twenty years ago, many of us were still living in the middle of regime change turmoil, replacing autocratic regimes with basic democratic rules. This is true for most of Europe, as well as many other countries across the globe – especially in South East Asia and Latin America. At that time we learned that democracy needs our active participation in order to become more of a reality. However, there was and is no blueprint as to how non-democratic countries can be transformed into democratic ones and how our democracies can become stronger and more sustainable – or simply spoken: more democratic!

But let's be very clear on one point: more democracy is never popular with those already in power, independently of whether they have been elected into office or not. The reason for this is that democracy not only means popular rule as a principle but also the separation of powers in practice. So what we need to learn together is how to shape our tools of democratization. We need in fact a much more fine-tuned separation of powers in the future – on all political levels, locally, regionally, nationally and transnationally. In order to be able to democratize our democracies we must make our representative political systems more representative – by introducing and strengthening the procedures and practices of modern direct democracy.

Modern direct democracy is a vigorously updated version of popular power. By overcoming the limitations of both classical assembly democracy like in ancient Athens or early parliamentary democracy – also known as the Westminster system – under which sovereignty was exercised by small groups of citizens or elected officials, we do in fact have possibilities to establish democracies for the globalized 21st century.

The new basic law of the European Union (EU), the Lisbon Treaty, which came into force in late 2009, does acknowledge this fundamental "new" paradigm. Namely, that modern direct democracy is an integrated part of representative democracy. Participative procedures, as outlined in the Lisbon Treaty under Art. 11.4 on the European Citizens' Initiative (ECI) will make representative democracy truly representative. Hence, EU citizenship is about to become a truly political citizenship; the Europeans are about to take responsibility in many ways: as electors in elections, agenda-setters, and decision-makers in popular votes on substantive issues. The shift towards a more truly representative democracy has also been acknowledged by the United Nations: in its 2009 "Guidance Note on Democracy", Secretary General Ban Ki-Moon has focused on the need for "full participation" by the citizens in decision-making processes, because "citizens' participation does not end with periodic elections".

This is indeed the time to develop our various people power "start-ups" across Europe and the world into a "super-democratic" framework – more direct and more transnational. Only a globalized super-democracy will be able to deal with the complex challenges and hurdles ahead by gradually democratizing all our political levels at hand and bringing in the citizens as the most important players. However, some still believe that a strong popular electorate will and should be able to replace the roles of political parties, parliaments or governments in a democracy; yet, under more direct and transnational forms of modern democracy, both elected and non-elected intermediaries will get even more important roles than today, not as decision-makers but as facilitators and communicators, prepared to assist all of us, the citizens, in our important role as agenda-setters and decision-makers on substantive issues.

Towards a universal language of modern direct democracy

Direct-democratic procedures have become key elements of a modern representative democracy. In many cases, however, as a result of unfavorable background conditions – such as limited freedom of information and lack of free expression of opinion, or impractical direct-democratic procedures – initiatives and referendums are not necessarily seen as a positive complement to representative democracy, but rather as a competitor or even a threat.

Well-designed and citizen-friendly direct-democratic procedures are, indeed, of critical importance at this time, as – beyond free and fair electoral processes – civic participation has become the key to sustainable democratic governance across the globe. In the last twenty years more than a hundred countries have in fact introduced institutional mechanisms of direct citizen participation within the framework of representative democracy. Other countries have experienced lawmaking by citizens for more than a century already. The growing use of initiative rights, popular votes on substantive issues and the mechanism for the recall of elected officials, have profoundly changed political dynamics.

When Europeans are soon empowered to launch transnational citizens' initiatives, Argentineans are gathering signatures to change the school law of their country, the people in Taiwan are voting on nuclear waste sites, Italians are gathering half a million signatures to put a parliamentary legislative act to a referendum – then we normally talk about the use of direct democracy. However, sometimes, in addition, votes to recall an elected official, like in Korea in late 2009, or a plebiscite that makes the unlimited re-election of a president possible, like in Venezuela, are put under the label of direct democracy. The world and the use of direct democracy have definitely grown dramatically under recent years.

All this creates a challenge to the use of language, classifications and terminology. As the number and use of direct democracy procedures are growing, the possibilities of confusions and misunderstandings do so as well. That is the reason why we need a universal coordinate system, covering all procedures of popular votes on substantive issues. This means that popular votes on persons and parties, for example, recall procedures, are NOT included. While the basic structure of the present classification is the result of a long-term developmental process, the implementation, practical use and operationalization are just about to begin. The basic structure of the grammar of modern direct democracy is based on the division of popular vote procedures into three different types: INITIATIVE, REFERENDUM and PLEBISCITE. The INITIATIVE comprises procedures where the author of the ballot proposal is THE SAME as the initiator of the procedure, the REFERENDUM procedures where the author of the ballot proposal is NOT the same as the initiator of the procedure. Finally the PLEBISCITE comprises procedures where the majority of a representative authority is both the author of the ballot proposal and the initiator of the procedure. However, procedures and practices exist which complicate this classification considerably and there are grey zones between the different types. With this in mind, the following is intended to guide you step-by-step through this introduction.

Three types and ten forms of modern direct democracy procedures

Popular vote procedures can be considered as political tools, of which different TYPES can be identified: INITIATIVE, REFERENDUM and PLEBISCITE. Just like a hammer or a screwdriver exists in different forms, INITIATIVE, REFERENDUM and PLEBISCITE also exist in different forms for different applications. One form of a REFERENDUM is for example a referendum triggered by law; another is a citizen-initiated referendum. In the following, the different forms of popular vote procedures and their characteristics will be described.

We use the term popular vote to designate a vote on a substantive political issue made by the voters, as opposed to a vote made by elected representatives. The term does not indicate what type the designated procedure is, and no particular definition of direct democracy is implied. So let us first address a few questions regarding this new typology, which was developed by the Initiative and Referendum Institute Europe during the first decade of the new millennium.

Question 1: What is a typology of popular vote procedures?

It is a classification of popular vote procedures into different types and forms that have characteristics in common.

Question 2: Why do we need such a typology?

On the one hand a typology is needed to avoid confusions in the discussions of direct democracy. Confusions arise when different types of procedures are given the same name, like when the word 'referendum' is used indistinguishably for authorities' controlled popular votes and for real referendums. Inversely a good deal of confusion results if the same procedure is given many different names, for example, if an agenda initiative is also called people's petition, popular initiative and people's proposition.

On the other hand, different countries use different juridical terminologies. Without a typology it is not possible to compare the repertoire of popular vote procedures between countries.

Question 3: What is the aim of our typology?

The aim of this typology is to classify the procedures in existence in a realistic and not merely formal way. The words 'initiative' and 'referendum' designate two different types of procedures whose use is controlled by minorities except for the obligatory referendum, which is determined by law. The word 'plebiscite' is used to designate a third type of procedure: authorities controlled popular votes (plebiscites). The distinction between referendums and authorities controlled popular votes is crucial: whereas referendums are tools of the people, plebiscites operate as tools of power holders for legitimization and mobilization or for bypassing other representative institutions or for disengaging from tough policies.

Question 4: What does this typology look like?

This classification of popular vote procedures only includes votes on substantive issues, not on people (like recall elections). It distinguishes popular vote procedures according to who is

1) the author of the ballot proposal (a group of citizens, a minority of a representative authority, a representative authority)
2) the initiator of the procedure (a group of citizens, law, a minority of a representative authority, a representative authority).
3) the decision-maker (the whole electorate, a representative authority).

In following table the forms of procedure are listed in column 1. The following columns indicate who is the author of the ballot proposal (column 2), who has the right to initiate the procedure (column 3), and who has the right to decide about the outcome of the procedure (column 4). The last column tells us about the TYPE of procedure in question. Citizen- and law-initiated procedures are in color (green for the initiative, yellow for the referendum) and procedures triggered by an authority are in grey.

Genuine direct democratic procedures are designed to offer the electorate instruments of agenda-setting and decision-making on substantive issues. However, in political reality, many procedures and especially practices of popular vote processes are partly or totally controlled by elected authorities. These mixed forms, which combine indirect and direct democracy, are indicated in our classification in grey colour. While forms initiated by a minority of an elected authority (e.g. 1/3 of parliament in Denmark or Sweden) are labeled under the INITIATIVE and the REFERENDUM type, procedures initiated by a majority of an elected authority are labeled under the PLEBISCITE type of popular vote procedures.

Abbreviations

The abbreviation for the form of procedure consists of 3 characters. The first character designates the initiator of the procedure (P = popular/citizens; A = authority; L = law) and the last character indicates the TYPE of procedure (I = INITIATIVE, R = REFERENDUM, P = PLEBISCITE). The middle character specifies the form of procedure (A = agenda, C = citizen, M = minority, O = obligatory, P = proposal, T = top-down). The "+" -sign indicates that the initiative or referendum procedure is combined with a counter-proposal.

Form of procedure

popular or citizens' initiative	PCI
citizens' initiative + counter-proposal	PCI+
agenda initiative	PAI
authorities' minority initiative	AMI
popular or citizen-initiated referendum	PCR
popular referendum + counter-proposal	PCR+
referendum proposal	PPR
authorities' minority referendum	AMR
obligatory referendum	LOR
plebiscite	ATP

Form	Author of the proposal	Initiator	Decision-maker	Type
citizens' or popular initiative	a group of citizens	the same group	the whole electorate	INITIATIVE
+ authorities' counter-proposal	a group of citizens	the same group	the whole electorate	INITIATIVE
agenda initiative	a group of citizens	the same group	a representative authority	INITIATIVE
authorities' minority initiative	minority of a representative authority	the same minority	the whole electorate	INITIATIVE
citizen-initiated or popular referendum	a representative authority	a group of citizens	the whole electorate	REFERENDUM
+ counter-proposal	a representative authority	a group of citizens	the whole electorate	REFERENDUM

referendum proposal	a representative authority	a group of citizens	a representative authority	REFERENDUM
obligatory referendum	a representative authority	law	the whole electorate	REFERENDUM
authorities' minority referendum	a representative authority	minority of a representative authority	the whole electorate	REFERENDUM
authorities' controlled popular vote / plebiscite	a representative authority	a representative authority	the whole electorate	PLEBISCITE

Agenda initiatives and referendum proposals are addressed to and decided by a representative authority; they may lead to a popular vote, but often they do not. Despite this, these two forms of procedure are included in our typology.

Three types and ten forms of popular vote procedures

Type 1. INITIATIVE

The right of a minority, normally a specified number of citizens, to propose to the public the introduction of a new or renewed law. The decision on the proposal is made through a popular vote.

Note that the agenda initiative fits into this type of procedure only with respect to its initial phase. What happens next is decided by a representative authority.

Form 1.1. PCI Citizens' Initiative (popular initiative)

The procedure is initiated by a prescribed number of eligible voters. The sponsors of a popular initiative can force a referendum vote on their proposal (assuming that their initiative is formally adopted); they may also withdraw their initiative (if there is a withdrawal clause).

This procedure may operate as a means of innovation and reform: it allows people to step on the gas pedal. In principle, initiatives enable people to get what they want.

Form I.2. PCI+ Citizens' initiative + authorities' counter-proposal

The authorities have the right to formulate a counter proposal within the framework of a popular initiative process. Both proposals are then decided on at the same time by popular vote. If both proposals are accepted, the decision on whether the original proposal or the parliament's counter-proposal should be implemented can be made by means of a special deciding question.

Form 1.3. PAI Agenda initiative (popular initiative proposal)

The agenda initiative is the right of a specified number of eligible voters to propose the adoption of a law or measure to a competent authority; the addressee of this proposal and request is not the whole electorate but a representative authority. In contrast to the popular initiative, it is this authority which decides what is going to happen to the proposal.

An agenda initiative can be institutionalized in a variety of ways: for example as an agenda initiative without popular vote, as an agenda initiative followed by a consultative or binding plebiscite or as a popular motion ("Volksmotion") The popular motion can be the equivalent of a parliamentary motion; if adopted, it can also be treated like a popular initiative (this is the case in the canton of Obwalden).

Form 1.4. AMI Authorities' minority initiative

Initiated by a minority of an authority (e.g. one third of the parliament), which can put its own proposal on the agenda and let the people decide on it.

Type 2. REFERENDUM

A direct democracy procedure which includes a popular vote on a substantive issue (ballot proposal) like, for example, a constitutional amendment or a bill; the voters have the right to either accept or reject the ballot proposal.

The procedure is triggered either by law (→ obligatory referendum) or by a specified number of citizens (→ popular referendum) respectively by a minority in an authority (→ authorities' minority referendum).

Form 2.1. PCR Popular or citizen-initiated referendum

The right of a specified number of citizens to initiate a referendum and let the whole electorate decide whether, for example, a particular law should be enacted or repealed. This procedure acts as a corrective to parliamentary decision-making in representative democracies and as a check on parliament and the government. The people (i.e. all those with the right to vote) have the right to decide in retrospect on decisions made by the legislature. Whereas the popular initiative works like a gas pedal, the popular referendum gives people the possibility to step on the brakes.

Form 2.2. PCR+ Popular referendum + counter-proposal

This procedure combines a popular referendum against a decision by an authority with a referendum on a counter proposal. If both proposals are accepted, the decision between the two can be made by means of a deciding question.

Form 2.3. PPR Referendum proposal

The right of a specified number of eligible voters to propose the calling of a popular vote; the proposal is addressed to a representative authority (usually parliament – local or national) which decides about further action.

Form 2.4. LOR Obligatory referendum

A law (usually the constitution) requires that certain issues must be put before the voters for approval or rejection. A conditional obligatory referendum means, that a specified issue must be put to the ballot only under certain conditions (e.g. if more than half but less than four fifth of the parliament accept the proposal). Unconditional referendums are without loophole.

Form 2.5. AMR Authorities’ minority referendum

The right of a minority in an authority to put a decision made by the majority in the same authority before the voters for approval or rejection. This procedure enables an authorities’ minority to step on the brakes and give the final say to the voters.

Type 3. PLEBISCITE

A public consultation controlled “from above”. It is the “powers that be” (the President, Prime Minister, Parliament) which decide when and on what subject the people will be asked to give their opinion. Such polls are frequently only consultative i.e. their results are not formally binding on parliament or government. In reality, plebiscites are instruments of power which those in power use in an attempt to reinforce or salvage that power with the help of the people. Their aim is not to implement democracy, but to provide a kind of legitimacy for decisions those in power have already taken.

Form 3.1. ATP Authority controlled popular vote (plebiscite)

A popular vote procedure whose use lies exclusively within the control of the authorities.

As we are entering the second decade of the new millennium, more and more citizens around the world are speaking out, adding their own questions to the political agenda and becoming increasingly involved in the decision-making process on substantive issues. Over the past 25 years participatory democracy has experienced an enormous boom. More than half of all the referendums and plebiscites ever held in history fall into this period. Only very few countries now remain in which there are no forms of direct-democratic participation at national or regional levels.

Nine out of ten countries or territories in the world now have one or more instruments of modern participatory democracy. These include partly the genuine direct-democratic right of initiative and referendum, but – in many countries – also the possibility of removing elected representatives before the end of their mandate (recall) or to hold a plebiscite, which is more an instrument of the rulers and not the citizens.

Unhelpful context, unfriendly design

The trend is clear: direct-democratic instruments are an essential part of today's representative democracy. In many cases, however, as a consequence of unhelpful and unfair background conditions – such as limited freedom of information and lack of free expression of opinion, or impractical direct-democratic procedures – initiatives and referendums are not necessarily seen as a positive complement to representative democracy, but rather as a competitor or even a threat.

For example, if a 50 percent turnout quorum is required before a referendum result can be declared valid, what frequently happens is that the usual "Yes" and "No" campaigns are joined by calls for a boycott. If the boycott action is successful, the "non-voters" will effectively be counted with the "no-voters", the turnout quorum will not be reached, and the democratic outcome will be perverted (the result of the vote is invalid, even if a clear majority of the actual voters have voted "Yes").

It can also happen that decidedly undemocratic regimes make use of the plebiscite and attempt to manipulate the opinion-forming and decision-making process by organising a "top-down" popular vote (perhaps bypassing an elected parliament). But problems can also occur when financially very powerful interest groups exploit initiative and referendum laws in the absence of compensating provisions which can help to ensure a free and fair referendum process.

As the countries with citizen-triggered popular votes illustrate, civil society groups are often the most highly motivated specialists for taking the development of democratic instruments forward and using them frequently and enthusiastically. The existence of an efficient interface between civil society and the authorities and the quality of the dialogue between them are of the highest importance. Worldwide, there is a growing emergence of civil society groups with a special focus on supporting and fostering the spread of direct-democratic tools, including some who already have considerable practical experience with them.

So, before refocusing on Europe and the new transnational, participative opportunities within the EU, let's have a brief look at the world of modern direct democracy:

Asia-Pacific

Asia is struggling with the strengthening of democratic forces after a period of autocratic backlash such as has been seen in Thailand, Malaysia and Bangladesh. However, there are plenty of opportunities around, especially but not only on the sub national level.

In Korea a series of domestic and international challenges and ideas, like the Free Trade Agreement with the issue or the plans to build a cross-country water conduit system were followed-up by a profound request for more participatory democracy. The same thing happened in Taiwan, where a Free Trade Agreement with China led to signature gathering campaigns trying to trigger a popular vote. In the Philippines and Thailand, existing procedures of modern direct democracy like the citizen initiative (PH) and the mandatory constitutional referendum (TH) were ingredients of a democratic reform debate, where in India, several states and many urban areas have introduced new forms of participatory – but not yet direct – democracy in recent years.

The new experiences made at the sub national level may encourage the possibility of a reform process at the federal level as well. Further south-east, several countries in Oceania have a wide range of direct-democratic provisions, including popular initiatives in New Zealand and mandatory constitutional referendums in Australia. In addition to this, many practical experiences have been reported from small island states such as Palau, Tokelau and New Caledonia, where the status of post-colonial autonomy and independence are issues to be decided by the electorate.

"People Power" has been the feature of "revolutions" in Asia before. Now millions of citizen across the region are trying to "evolute" this concept into concrete reform programmes. In the Philippines the forthcoming presidential election in May 2010 will probably see the return of reform-minded administration under "Noynoy" Aquino, the son of Cory Aquino, who died in late 2009.

Americas

Across the Pacific Ocean, many US states have seen dozens of citizens' initiatives ("propositions") which made it to the ballot box along with the recent election cycle in late 2009. As before many groups used initiatives to try to produce spin-off effects for their candidate or their issue. In California, among other issues, planning (California Property Owner and Farmland Protection Act), transportation (funding), high-speed railways, education (funding) and new taxes (on wealth) were at the ballot. Another important issue was the vote on gay marriage, which was deemed legal and allowed by a court decision in spring. In Oregon, voters got the last word on a building law (Measure 49) and a constitutional amendment to fund health care for children. Further north, the citizens of the Canadian province of British Columbia vote a second time in four years on a proposed change of their electoral system from the (UK-style) first-past-the-post to a single transferable vote system. And again, the reform vote failed. In Ontario, a similar process to change into a mixed-member proportional system led to a referendum on October 10, 2007. In this historic vote (the first popular vote on a substantive issue in the state since 1921), Ontarians opted for the status quo. The existing first-past-the-post system got 63.3% of the ballots; the turnout reached 53%.

In Latin America, the 1980s were characterized by the return to civilian government after prolonged periods of authoritarian military rule. However, the hopes of many people that representative democracy would better serve their interests were disappointed and discontent with the political parties and representative government grew. This disappointment of broad parts of the population contributed to the emergence of direct democracy in Latin America as had happened in Switzerland in the second half of the 19th century and in the USA around the turn to the 20th century. However, strong popular demands for direct democracy are not widespread, except in Bolivia. In Latin America most of the new constitutions adopted since the late 1980s included direct democratic rights, but also plebiscites and sometimes the right to recall (e.g. in Bolivia, Colombia, Peru, and Venezuela).

Africa

Across Africa many countries have inherited some basic principles and forms of direct democracy from their former colonial powers. This is especially true for most former French colonies in Western Africa, where referendums "from above" (French-style plebiscites) are both part of the constitutional arrangements and – more seldom – also of political practice. But there is also another growing practice of instituting referendums, as in

South Africa, the Democratic Republic of the Congo, Zambia and Madagascar which has made a significant contribution to greater democratic stability. In the north of the African continent, strong Islamic leaders have misused the referendum instrument in many ways. In 2007, Egyptian president Hosni Mubarak offered the people just 7 days to discuss and agree on a list of 34 constitutional amendments. Less than 30% of the registered voters took part in the plebiscite. Despite such experiences, which lie outside a free and fair framework, many Africans forecast a much more frequent use of direct-democratic instruments in the near future: the Eastern African Community – a regional intergovernmental organisation with five member states – plans a transnational referendum, to be held at some time after 2010, on the establishment of a political union in East Africa. An even more extensive direct-democratic event is envisaged by the Pan-African Council and the All-African People's Organisation: they have called for a pan-African popular vote on a union government for 53 states with more than 800 million people.

Europe

The majority of direct-democratic events are, however, still reported from Europe, where most countries today have initiative and referendum processes at least on the local and/or regional levels. At the other end of the spectrum, the 27-member European Union is deeply involved in a development which will bring the citizens onto the political stage transnationally as well. Since far more than half of all national legislation now has its origin at the European level, a transfer of participatory democratic instruments to the relevant legislative level becomes a key reform necessity. This is not so easy in practice, since the idea of national and popular sovereignty frequently clashes with the need to make Europe more democratic. Nevertheless, the ongoing constitutional debate in Europe has produced many transnational activities which may impress even long-term critics of the European integration process.

Already back in 2004, the EU heads of state and government agreed to include the principle of direct democracy in the then-proposed constitutional treaty. While the "constitution" did not pass the referendum test in all member states – the French and Dutch voted against it – the participatory principle survived to become part of the Lisbon Treaty, which will be put into force on December 1, 2009. Article 11.4 of the Lisbon Treaty provides for the right of one million EU citizens to propose a new European law or regulation.

This is an agenda initiative right, which to begin with will have no possibility of triggering a pan-European popular vote. But even before any implementing regulation had been drafted, at least 20 transnational European Citizens' Initiatives were launched between 2006 and 2008, addressing issues such as human rights, energy and European democracy.

A brief assessment of these twenty pilot initiatives shows that the new instrument is being used by many different groups from different sectors of society including politicians, human rights groups, conservative organizations, economic foundations and broad alliances of non-governmental groups. However, since the concept of the European Citizens' Initiative is still new, and since the culture and practice of initiative is at present weakly developed in many European countries, several initiatives are still calling their attempt to gather one million signatures a "petition".

Furthermore, the fact that the implementation regulation does not yet exist means that all kinds of ways of collecting signatures are being used, including the simple registration of names online without clear verifiability. At the same time, it is clear that the Internet offers a unique transnational platform for launching and conducting such initiatives. Interestingly, most of the initiatives so far launched understand the need to publish their information in as many European languages as possible.

This dynamic development of transnational direct-democratic practice offers many opportunities, both for academics and political practitioners, to test and assess the first steps towards transnational direct democracy. In the near future, however, it will be essential to carefully establish a democratic infrastructure beyond the raw tool of the initiative. This will include some kind of European electoral management body to assist, test and follow up European Citizens' Initiatives, as well as implementing a comprehensive voter education programme across the region.

In the last decade, Europe has made its first steps towards becoming a modern transnational democracy. The integration process offers a prime and unique case study of practical democratization beyond the nation state – and hence a first view of what is likely to happen around the globe in other contexts as well. This direct democratic experience includes almost 50 country-wide popular votes on European issues in 27 European countries.

With so many popular votes in so many different countries over such a long time, the effects of having popular votes on Europe in Europe have recently been the subject of extensive research projects. The results of these comparative and empirical studies are highly encouraging. Citizens in charge of important decisions become far better informed than people without such voting opportunities. Moreover, a team at the European University Institute of Florence has shown that referendum votes on Europe in Europe predominantly deal with the subject matter in hand: "Direct democracy has fostered a high degree of politicisation of integration", according to political scientists Andrew Glencross and Alexander Trechsel.

Under reasonably well-designed and citizen-friendly circumstances, direct-democratic procedures can deliver precisely what a quasi-transnational polity such as the EU most lacks today: an intense dialogue between institutions and citizens, a feeling of ownership of EU politics by the voters, and solid legitimacy for the decisions made at EU level.

However, all forms of transnational direct democracy must of course be embedded in wider contexts such as basic human and civil rights, the rule of law, regional and possibly overlapping transnational entities, manifold levels of autonomy, as well as the structures for and assistance to deliberative processes beyond national borders.

In contrast to the local and national levels, where a broad set of direct-democratic instruments is already known and (mis)used, for the European level it make sense to begin with a starter set of initiative and referendum instruments. The new European Citizens' Initiative offers a new avenue and can – if implemented in a careful and citizen-friendly manner – become the first standard-bearer of 21th century super-democracy!

Michael EFLER

European Citizens' Initiative

Legal Nature and Criteria for Implementation

Introduction

Article 11.4 of the Draft Treaty on European Union (amended by Treaty of Lisbon) creates for the very first time a transnational tool of direct democracy.

It reads: *"Not less than one million citizens who are nationals of a significant number of Member States may take the initiative of inviting the European Commission, within the framework of its powers, to submit any appropriate proposal on matters where citizens consider that a legal act of the Union is required for the purpose of implementing the Treaties. The procedures and conditions required for such a citizens' initiative shall be determined in accordance with the first paragraph of Article 21 of the Treaty on the Functioning of the European Union."*

The aim of this paper is to contribute to the development of criteria for the "procedures and conditions required for such a citizens' initiative". It also tries to clarify the legal nature of the ECI. This paper is the result of the work of an independent expert group that met six times to discuss the main structural elements of such procedures and conditions. This group was coordinated by Bruno Kaufmann (Initiative & Referendum Institute Europe) and Michael Efler (democracy international).

This paper shall also contribute to the efforts of the European Parliament to work out a report on the implementation of the ECI.

Legal nature of ECI

It is imperative that the nature of the ECI is initially defined.[1] The ECI allows citizens to ask (or "invite") the Commission to start a legislative process.

1 The following remarks are based on the wording of Art 11.4 draft Treaty on European Union. They may not be valid if this wording will be changed.

This wording leaves open the legal nature of the ECI. It has already created some confusion among analysts of ECI regarding the role of the European Commission.

It is quite clear that the ECI is non-binding for the Commission in the sense that it has to submit the ECI proposal unchanged to the Parliament and the Council.[2] This would not be in line with the Commission's monopoly of legislative initiative and the wording of Art 11.4. However according to the majority view of European law experts and the "effet utile" of the ECI, it has a binding nature for the Commission in the sense that it has to take some legislative action on the topic proposed by the ECI. The precondition is that the ECI is declared admissible.[3]

It would be a misuse of citizens' resources if the gathering of one million signatures would be without any consequence for the Commission. The very intention of the ECI is to give the citizens more influence on EU politics. It is therefore necessary that an admissible ECI has some result. This is not a contradiction to the Commission's initiative monopoly, as the Commission is not strictly bound by the content of the ECI. In this respect, it is very important that Art. 192.2 TEC was the model for the drafting of Art. 11.4.[4] Art. 192.2 creates a "right of initiative for an initiative" or "indirect initiative right" for the European Parliament. This is a binding right. The Commission has to present a draft legal act, but is flexible regarding the timing and the content of its proposal. If the Commission refuses to act, the Parliament could take action for failure to act.[5] The same applies to Art. 208 TEC that gives the Council an indirect initiative right.[6] The obligation of the Commission is somewhat similar to the obligations Member

2 Only Cuesta, op. cit., p. 72, seems to agree with a limited role of the Commission: *"...once the initiative has satisfied these requirements, the popular request should be automatically passed on by the Commission to the lawmaking process."*

3 Epiney, A.: Europäische Verfassung und Legitimation durch die Unionsbürger – Zu den Rechten der Unionsbürger in der Verfassung für Europa, in Kadelbach, S. (ed.): Europäische Verfassung und direkte Demokratie, 2006, pp. 49-52, citing supporting evidence and Fischer, K.-H.: Der Europäische Verfassungsvertrag, 2005, p. 202 (views the ECI as a breach of the initiative monopoly of the Commission).

4 Meyer, J.: Questions & Answers about the new citizens right, in Filliez, F./Kaufmann, B. (eds.): The European Constitution – Bringing in the people, Contributions on "The options and limits of direct democracy in the European integration process", 2004, p. 26.

5 Kaufmann-Bühler, W., in Lenz, C.-O./Borchardt, K.-D. (eds.): EU- und EG-Vertrag, Kommentar, 2006, Art. 192 EGV, RN 9-10; Epiney, op. cit., pp. 49-52 citing supporting evidence; Kluth, op. cit., Art. 192, RN 9-11 citing supporting evidence (refusing only the interpretation that the Parliament could make a complaint for failure to act).

6 Kaufmann-Bühler, op. cit., RN 2; Epiney, op. cit., p. 52 citing supporting evidence; Kluth, op. cit., Art. 208, RN 3-4 citing supporting evidence, but also citing one dissenting opinion.

States have with respect to directives: they are binding, as to the result to be achieved, but the choice of form and methods is left open to the national authorities (Art. 249 TEC). Analogously, the ECI has the same legal consequence. The Commission is obliged to take legislative action once the required number of signatures has been attained and the ECI is declared admissible.

In any case, it is not possible to bind the Parliament or the Council because only the Commission is the recipient of the ECI. Even if the Commission fully approves an ECI, there is no guarantee that it will ever enter into force. If the Parliament and the Council do not act, there is no possibility of a referendum on the ECI. This is different from the Swiss-style popular initiatives.

Recommendations for an ECI implementation legislation

1. Treaty amendments included?

The specific wording of Art. 11.4: "for the purpose of implementing the Treaties", leaves some room for the interpretation that the ECI could not be used to propose treaty amendments. But this would be a major shortcoming. It was never the intention of the drafters of Art. 11.4 to limit the ECI to a statutory initiative. Art. 192.2 TEC – the model of Art. 11.4 – is not reduced to secondary law initiatives. Furthermore, the Lisbon Treaty is more complex and regulates much more policy content than e.g. national constitutions do. Excluding treaty amendments would prevent European citizens from participating in the most important policy fields. Art. 48.2 of the Draft Treaty on European Union enables the European Commission and – for the first time – the European Parliament to propose amendments of the Treaties. Why shouldn't the citizens of Europe be able to ask the Commission to propose such amendments?

Recommendation: The implementing legislation should make it clear that treaty amendments can be proposed by an ECI.

2. Not more than one million citizens

"Not less than one million citizens" have to give their signatures for an ECI. This is a lower hurdle than that in the majority of the nine national constitutions of old and new EU Member States which provide for citizens' initiatives. Only the Italian constitution has a lower relative number of required signatures. The collection of one million signatures – in a significant number of Member States (see next point) – just to ask the Commission to act is already a high hurdle.

Recommendation: The required minimum number of signatures to be gathered should not exceed one million.

3. A significant number of member states

This condition is designed to guarantee the "European" character of an ECI. It seems doubtful if such a condition is really necessary – but this issue is decided by the very text of Art. 11.4. The legislator should take care that this requirement does not impose too high hurdles for an effective implementation of the ECI. A European civil society is only just in the making.

Recommendation: The number of "significant" member states should be 4.

4. Minimum number of signatures that must be collected in each country

It would be very logical to set a minimum number of signatures to come from each of the 4 countries. Otherwise it would be enough to collect just one signature in the other countries to fulfill this requirement.

Recommendation: The required minimum number of signatures that come from each of the countries (a minimum of 4, as above) should be 0.1% of the citizens entitled to vote.

5. Time period for collection of signatures

A short time period would put the initiative under extreme pressure and would disadvantage smaller groups. So it would be desirable to set a relatively long time period. It is important that signatures can be freely collected (in all public spaces).

Recommendation: The time period for the collection of signatures should not be more than 18 months.

6. Formal requirements of the proposal

Should the proposal take the form of a general initiative which has to be formulated in legal terms by the Commission – or should the citizens present a formal draft legal act (Art. 288 Draft Treaty on the Functioning of the European Union) to the Commission? The former would give the Commission an important role because the "devil is always in the details". European NGOs and political parties – which will be the primary users of the ECI – have the capacity and capability to draft laws and other European legal acts. But it could be wise to let the initiators themselves decide on the form of an ECI. If they choose a general proposal, then they should state the specific goal(s) of the legislation and the main measures to be introduced (or changed).

Recommendation: An ECI may be presented in the form of a draft legal act or as a general proposal.

7. Role of the Commission

It is obvious that the Commission has to check whether the requirements of the ECI (number of signatures, number of countries involved etc.) have been met. An examination as to whether the proposal respects the boundaries of the European competences and the Charter of Fundamental Rights seems necessary. The initiators should have the right to challenge a rejection (by the Commission) before the European Court of Justice.

Recommendation: The Commission has to check whether the formal conditions of the ECI have been fulfilled and that no conflict with European law exists. The Commission has to give its reasons in case of rejection. This decision could be appealed by the initiators. There should be strict time limits for the subsequent treatment of the subject by the EU institutions.

8. Rights of the Initiative

The initiative (represented by an initiative committee) should have the right to be heard by the respective institutions (the Commission; in the event of the initiation of the lawmaking process, the Parliament and the European Council). As mentioned above, it should have the right to challenge a negative decision by the Commission. A reimbursement in part of the costs for the initiative campaign seems appropriate. The specific details have to be worked out. The initiative should have the possibility, but not the obligation, to ask the European Commission, before the launch of an ECI, whether its proposal is in compliance with European Law (right of advice). The Commission would be obliged to give an answer to that application and should also help the initiative to draft an ECI. In addition, the Commission should be obliged to publish without delay the text of the ECI in the Official Journal of the European Union and in the Official Gazettes of Member States.

Recommendation: The initiative should have the right to be heard by the respective institutions, to get adequate reimbursement and a right of advice from the European Commission. The text should be published in the official journals of the EU and the member states.

9. How should the European law define "citizens who are nationals" and who should verify the signatures?

The first question is already decided by the very fact that only the Member States themselves can decide about the question of nationality. Verification should be organized by the Member States for practical reasons.

Recommendation: The question of verification of signatures should be decided by the member states according to their national electoral laws.

10. Free collection of signatures

It should be specified that the signatures could be gathered freely (by circulation/downloading of lists to be filled in and signed) and not only in government registration offices. This is very important to increase the communication among the citizens – within the Member States and within the whole EU. In this respect a uniform collection method has to be created by the implementing law.

Recommendation: It should be specified that the signatures could be gathered freely.

Anne-Marie SIGMUND

A Decesive Step Towards a Modern European Model of Democracy

Even though the final text of the Lisbon Treaty has failed to meet expectations of many convent participants (including my own!) in its stipulations regarding democratic principles, it nonetheless remains a very decisive step towards a modern European model of democracy. True, the much discussed civil dialogue is not named expressis verbis, yet has its constitutional foundation henceforth in Para 1 (horizontal dialogue) and 2 (vertical dialogue) of Article 11 TEUnv. I also see it as progress that the consultation practice of the Commission now has a constitutional reference in Para 3 of Article 11.

The great future potential however lies in Para 4 of Article 11: "a minimum of 1 million" Union citizens are given the right pending certain requirements to address the Commission with a proposal and thus hold – besides the right to petition the European Parliament according to Article 44 of the EU Charta – a further fundamental democratic element in their hands. Much, if not all will now depend on how much and in which form the Commission now puts this constitutional task into practice in its legislation for implementation. The expected ordinance will have a whole catalogue of content-related questions to answer and will need to look at procedure-technical problems. And I believe that, as is the case so often, the devil will be found in the details. According to the hearing, the Commission will carry out a consultation procedure before presenting the ordinance which will offer the opportunity to all those interested to contribute their specific knowledge and their experience to this innovative process. I assume that the "European Citizens Initiative Office" which is being constituted here in Salzburg will also take part in this procedure.

The European Economic and Social Committee will devise an initiative commentary on this project, which I will mentor in the role of correspondent. Without wishing to abort our further discussion, I would like to broadly sketch out what I feel are the essential points:

As a recognized aspect henceforth of democratic foundational rights of Union citizens, the European Citizens' Initiative is a historic step in the history of European integration, since it allows the transnational element to flow into the European democracy mode and paves the way for a truly existent European public entity, which is of itself an inalienable prerequisite for the creating and operating of European citizens who acclaim their European identity.

It is of great importance to undertake a clean separation between indirect/representative democracy, which is the main pillar of European democratic actions, and direct/participatory democracy:

The European Citizens' Initiative, according to Article 11.4 TEU, is a new political decision-making procedure with strong participation of the populace which augments the European democracy model with a new element which complements the representative element – independent of it! – but does not replace it.

The European Parliament is the mandate bearer of representative democracy at the European level; it can support the participative element of the European democratic model but cannot control it.

Mistakable interpretation of the legitimation basis for political action is to be avoided. Based on the fact that legitimate action is to be understood as lawful action in the context of an assigned task, it is my view that it is an absolute moot point to demand that every exercising of political rights in the context of the European democracy model be based on polls. It is self evident that each representative who takes part in the legislative process through his or her vote should be able to rely upon an orderly voting result. This however does not apply for those representatives of civil society taking part in a public political opinion-forming process.

The consultation procedure which is described in Art 11.3 can take place in the context of the representative as well as the participative democracy, it is an additive element in the political formation of opinion but not exclusively definitive for one of the two democracy models, which indeed in themselves do not exclude either but complement the other.

It must not be forgotten to take the financial aspect of the European Citizens' Initiative into account. I would find it a serious injury to the principle of equality if only Citizens' Initiatives which – for whatever reasons – have access to independent financial resources were allowed to take part in the procedure; I think it is inalienable that collaborative financial contexts be envisaged for initiatives which promise success.

Johannes W. PICHLER

Recommendations to Initiatives – and to the EU as well

I.

Europeans have not recognized until now that there is a new direct democratic instrument under way, for that matter, a tremendous step into the future. It is a first transnational, direct democratic step – this is a new landmark in the political history of humankind. The media, which actually should have noticed it are nevertheless either uninformed or ignorant – or, worst case, suppress the information for a reason and rational I don't know. Quartum non datur.

Who could make the turnabout? The EU itself, quite evidently, since no one else can. The climatic turn of tides must come top down this time. This top-down model cannot be the first choice for a direct democrat, of course, but the end justifies the means, at least as an exception in our case. So the EU is invited to provoke the Europeans to come up with their real concerns. I call upon the Commission: channel the concerned and proactive citizens right through your door. Karim Giese and I have written a short, simple and clear model (We Change Europe, 179pp) of a proposition for a European initiative procedure, well-founded upon a legal comparison of nearly all European laws on national initiative rights. This includes recommendations to the EU authorities on how to design regulations so that the Initiative Right will not be a stillborn law but a vital and flourishing entity. I recommend to the EU responsible authorities that they reflect upon these valuable examples of rationality. And, further, Commission, please keep in mind what we are talking about in actuality. We are talking about a preliminary stage preparation instrument. The Initiative Right under Art 11.4 TEU can do no more and does not want to do more than to create an indirect initiative – an agenda setting initiative. Basically, nothing can ever be forced or overruled through using initiatives. At the end of the day, it is always and will remain the Commission which dominates the whole process of this kind of direct democracy. So:

II.

Commission, be wise! Commission, act open-mindedly! Do not fool around with wimpy legal hindrances on the admissibility of an initiative based on this or that artificial clause like what is being batted around regarding the so-called "constitutional initiatives". Why use this example, which was dealt with so strongly within the European Parliament? Because this is a classical entrapment that could make Europeans upset. What's the minimal and thin rationale behind the argument? Some, mostly lawyers, as always, say, it is beyond the Commission's competence to initiate a Treaty reform and therefore citizens are not entitled to conduct an initiative on something of that kind, as though this competence were found exclusively within in the Member States. And thus out of reach of the Commission and even more so of the average citizens.

A clear misreading, in my humble opinion. The Commission is a political entity. It can bargain on anything whatsoever. And how did the Parliament react to that kind of interpretation? Imagine, the Committee on Constitutional Affairs fiddled around with this point, but has not at all signalized any significant protest. To the contrary, the Committee has played with the idea to call for another, a second Initiative Right, a Constitutional Initiative Right. To whom should such initiatives be addressed? Guess! No, not to the Commission, this time. In that case, it should be addressed to the Parliament. So the Parliament takes this opportunity to philosophize about a new competence for itself! Can one imagine what this legal barrier, namely excluding constitutional Initiatives, implies: European citizens should not be allowed to launch constitutional concerns! They are forbidden to come up with initiatives on such topics. Unbelievable. In what world do the EU professionals actually live? We, the Europeans, are the sovereign. And they will cut off the use of our fundamental rights? Strange. So here is a key point for the Resolution: to invite a clear statement by the Commission and the Council insisting that this interpretation of Parliament is wrong in essence and that initiatives are most welcome to come up with any initiative, even ones proposing change and further development of constitutional treaties – the Treaty of Lisbon is clearly this type. Let's get over that. And let's hope that the Commission comes through with more political fantasy in favor of the citizens.

III.

Initiatives, be seriously political! Do not fuss with opaque, illusive and diffuse general concerns. Every initiative needs to have a clear political issue. This purpose-related task is to be handled exclusively by the initiators themselves and by no one else. Creators of initiatives should not seek advice concerning which issues are best for them, even when the source is a political market specialist. But let me propose the first crucial point right here. Having the right idea as insisted above is only a preliminary step: the real problems are yet to come.

IV.

Nonetheless, it would be good to be sufficiently equipped and to be able to afford research to review the standing of the issue. Initiatives, you need certainty about your standing and about your chances to attract a lot of citizens. I am sardonically provocative now. Unless your goal is just to brand an issue (and burn it) and you are committed in any case, never go after the required minimum of a million votes as is required under the often mentioned Art 11.4 TEU nv/Treaty of Lisbon.

V.

Initiatives should answer the following three questions, first directed to the public in general, and then to the EU in particular. These questions are:

1. What is going wrong that will be resolved by this initiative?
2. How will your initiative resolve the problem?
3. Why should I, as a voter, support rather than oppose you?

If these questions cannot be answered clearly and convincingly, then it would be advisable to keep out of that political battle. In reflecting on the background of my own initiatives, I had, and I still have, three convincing answers so I will press on – and I think, once Europeans are informed, they should be convinced as well. It is to everyone's benefit to make every concerned European voice heard. Believe me, Obama's message of "Yes, we can" will be well received in good old placid Europe. My personal initiatives' obstacle seems to be with the procedure rather than its worth.

VI.

Despite my bad experiences, I still would recommend that Initiatives&Initiators partner with a highly reputable campaigning firm from the start. For pure idealists, this is not an easy proposition because there is cost and the risk of locating the wrong ones, as I did. Let me make my second general point right here, addressed to the EU authorities. It is inevitable that there will one day be an independent agency, outsourced but under the umbrella of the EU, which will monitor such firms and post them on an internal blacklist for inappropriateness. How it insures that this type of impartial agency is put into place is the first gauge of whether or not the EU takes the Initiative Right seriously.

VII.

Initiative organizers should not contract with any campaigners or fundraisers who are not willing to outline their concepts and strategy in detail. If the campaigners refuse, they should walk out immediately. The aforementioned agency or office should also work to get its hands on this problem. There could be an accreditation scheme, a certification scheme or similar, carried out and administered by this entity.

VIII.

One of the DOs and DON'Ts I learned regarding the campaigning literature I have used in our book "We Change Europe" is that an initiative should not only launch an online campaign but should use traditional offline channels as well. I trusted in my own research and therefore spent too much time and money with the offline period, which was the wrong decision. The literature promoting a combo campaign is not up-to-date. Obama proved that, and he won finally by using the Internet.

So, if any campaigner recommends starting with an offline campaign, tell him to go to hell because the opposite is true. Every European initiative must be carried out as an eCampaign right from the beginning otherwise time is wasted and money burned, as I well know from experience. Let me make my third point: if the EU is committed to transforming the existing political anger among so many Europeans with direct democracy, it must (!) come up with a valid model and good tools for eCampaigns and serve with that – for free of course. I offer all of my knowledge to the public and to the EU in how to design this kind of tool. Moreover, until the EU provides us with tools like this, I invite initiative people to use our tool for the pre-campaigning phase. Just contact "we-change-europe.eu".

IX.

Budget planning is the most crucial element of any initiative. There is no experience available on how to do this. Proof of that? All political parties in Europe are deeply in debt because the campaigning budgets spin out of control on a regular basis. There is always this or that to add on, something to include, a question to answer, something to make better, etc. – and these unforeseen revisions always make campaigning expensive. Why presume that initiatives will not face the same fatal end? They will, as we did. So the next lesson to be drawn is that initiatives must have consultation from an impartial institution. And to that end again, I have no other recommendation than that the EU create a consulting agency or office for initiatives from the start.

X.

Fundraising is a widely unknown field in Europe compared to the US. There are fundraising organizations under way but their experience lies mainly with charities. Political parties have their supporters but even they are orphans compared to American parties. And, let's not forget that political parties' supporters are hardly philanthropists. Donations of that kind are mainly for lobbying purposes. European initiatives need to prove that they are not hiding a lobby and have a long way to go until they will receive significant funding from individuals or impartial foundations. In Europe, politics unfortunately connotes negative emotions and impressions. Therefore, the fourth and next lesson to be learned is this: without public support and funding, initiatives will be not successful. Again, a bit sardonically: if the EU does not want to see initiatives successful, all it has to do is do nothing to support them and it will succeed.

XI.

There will never ever be any success without the media. That's true. From our experience we have learned that European Initiatives must face another hard fact: the media – the paid media are unaffordable for normal citizens and are not dedicated to the citizens. The opposite appears to be true: they are – very quietly – linked to the real powers and interests. This was the greatest surprise to me. I always thought that the media would jump on our bandwagon immediately when honest European citizens stood up as volunteers, unpaid and without recognition, in order to contribute to Europeanizing the Europeans. Hardly!

As I mentioned in my experience, despite an information campaign carried out by top professionals with connections to all the networks, there was no response from the media. A lousy issue? Or just a lousy no-name representative of the issue? The first question cannot be answered but the second one can certainly – with yes. But is this reason enough not to disseminate information that eventually could thrill citizens concerned with the EU? I admit to being fully helpless with no wisdom on what concerns the traditional media. The EU itself is presented by the media as an oxymoron. Witness only how many millions of Euros the Information Commissioner has invested in its information policy which did not receive any significant attention from the media at all, not to mention presenting the EU in a significantly better light. To the contrary, the media worried even more that this EU money for top down information had been thrown out the window. So, since a media policy is crucial for the fate of European initiatives, I would recommend that we discuss here how to better use the Internet to attract the web 2.0 community because there are new media underway and we ourselves are the journalists now. And if we succeed in making the European citizens aware that there is something in their interest and to their benefit, then the traditional media will follow on their own.

XII.

To come to an end, I will sum up what is needed and what is not.

Firstly, to give future initiatives a chance to become successful, we do urge the creation of a seamless chain of support by the EU. Support also means the elimination of barriers and hindrances.

Secondly, a guiding, consulting, advising institution must immediately be formed. This entity is to be structured as a fully independent organization, best based within a non-profit and experienced institution.

Thirdly, it is a serious provocation that the Parliament requires a transparency principle for initiatives, which, on the other hand – again within the concept of Parliament – does not get supported with public money. As long as we are without a law that guarantees perfect transparency in regards to which part of the gigantic lobbying industries intimates what to a Commissioner, it is inacceptable to require a total transparency of initiatives. Let's bargain, Commission! Support initiatives with a public financing scheme – and then, of course, insist on a disclosure principle. But only then!

Fourthly, break with the almost endless chain of requirements. Commission, Council, ignore this part of the Report of the Parliament. They have not shown themselves citizen-friendly at all. Commission, make a significant change. Come up with your own proposal. Delight the people, surprise them. Provide an office de liaison for permanent contact with each and every initiative. We recommend that you ask the European Economic and Social Council to act as a permanent moderator or mediator between you and initiatives.

If these conditions were all to be heard, it would be much easier to collect one or more millions. And the Commission, in return, should welcome the chance to come in touch with Europeans directly.

Believe me, Commission, you may be at risk due to many of your "partners", but not from democratically active citizens.

Karim GIESE

Statement on the Initiative-Summit-Resolution

I.

The European authorities have recognized the need to bring the European Community closer to the citizens of the Member States on several occasions. In order to maintain and foster an open, transparent and on-going dialogue with the civil society until now, special financial European "programs to promote active European citizenship" have especially enabled (already well-) organized civil society to be able to operate und cooperate at the European level and participate in policy-making through consultation.

II.

With the European Citizens' Initiative, there is a realistic chance to also give the possibility of direct participation in European policy-making to the not or not as well (as in ad-hoc, "temporarily") organized civil society. The right to an initiative as the "softest" instrument of direct democracy is an integral part of the political systems today within the Member States and, under certain circumstances, direct democracy can become quite vital as we see at the moment for example in Germany. In Hamburg, citizens take up position against the privatization of hospitals; in Berlin, they demand school lessons in religion; in Thuringia, they have already enforced a better design of direct democracy; in Brandenburg, citizens are concerned with special problems in industry, in Bavaria, citizens have even changed the state organisation successfully. The fact that there is also a need for initiatives at the European level becomes quite evident when we regard the multitude of current European Citizens' Initiatives "avant la lettre".

III.

Whether or not the European Citizens' Initiative will be able to fulfil the citizens' expectations as a "place for amateurs" (in form of "grassroots"-initiatives) depends – as the different experiences within the Member States demonstrate – essentially on its legal "design" as well as on the supportive (or contra productive) cultural, technical and economic backgrounds.

The fact that the design determines which – established or non-established – actors may make use of the European Citizens' Initiative is very clear. The number of support declarations, the necessary geographical distribution, the time span and method to collect support declarations may cause unsolvable problems for insufficiently-organized actors (without any special networks for mobilisation of citizens). It is not easy even in Switzerland (heralded as direct democracy's avant-garde) for organized civil society to collect the necessary 100,000 support declarations for a national initiative among its own members. Thus it becomes clear why, in German Baden-Württemberg, for example, where more than one million citizens have to sign petitions within two weeks in the offices of the local authorities, there has never been a single attempt made to organize the first citizens' initiative.

IV.

For initiatives at the European level, the principle of representation undoubtedly needs a higher number of support declarations und a particular minimum of necessary geographical distribution. But even if we could assume a fairly strong interest by citizens to participate in the European political process, this type of "high-level" direct democracy process also needs a better supportive (technical and economic) framework than usual (i.e. in the Member States). As the developments in the USA show, only the highly professional guidance and support of a modern campaign industry (utilizing paid publicity or modern communication technologies – see "MyBarackObama.com") is able to produce the necessary dynamics in the field of direct democracy. High costs go along with this support and have to be financed by donations. Neither is – seen realistically – (also in the USA) to be had in the case of agenda-setting-initiatives only (in the mode of the European Citizens' Initiative).

V.

So if the European Community Initiative is to really become a vital element at the European level used by ad-hoc, "temporarily" organized citizens, it certainly needs two ("institutional") supplementary provisions to strengthen the process of European initiatives. These supplementary provisions don't have to be invented since they are not absolutely new. Member States which take direct democracy more seriously than others have already developed comparable provisions at the national (regional) level:

1. Formally registered initiatives (and only these) guarantee a special quality and the seriousness of the initiative-process. Such initiatives have

to become known to European citizens on a central (digital) platform which is just as serious and well organized. As we know, in contrast to the USA, political activities of citizens in the “free” virtual space of internet are not as common in Europe until now.

For this task (and others), an “ECI Agency” needs to be established under the general supervision of the European Commission. And this agency should also give the necessary advice and support to European initiatives (comparable to “MoveOn” in the USA). Advice must mean – as is common and standard as well in some Member States today – to help to solve juridical questions (e.g. concerning all the formal aspects of initiatives), but there should also be professional help (on the basis of general experiences) in fundamental and practical questions concerning campaigning, collecting donations, etc. This leads as well to questions of further technical and other support. An agency of this sort must give initiatives a virtual (internet-) platform (e.g. space for chat rooms), make special software-programs available (à la “Partybuilder”) etc – this could also save a lot of money (for parallel “private” internet-presentations). And, personally, I think that there should also be special services available for translation. If initiatives are to find transnational support, these initiatives must be presented in the most important European languages just as is matter of course within the European Community and its institutions.

2. The costs of an average European initiative cannot be predicted at the moment. But even in Switzerland, it can be necessary for quite well-organized associations to raise € 700,000 only to mobilize their own members (using internet communication) and to achieve support from 100,000 citizens. In California/USA, the campaign industry estimates that the average costs for getting the initial prerequisite support declarations at up to two million dollars: These are costs which initiatives in Europe cannot finance with only the small donations of concerned citizens. Thus, if the European Citizens' Initiatives is not to end up a playground for the already well-organized civil society and strong lobby-groups (as in the USA), it undoubtedly also needs a system of financial support. Some Member States have already started to give remunerations to all (successful) initiatives. In part, the remunerations are based on an overall amount (from € 11,000 – Austria – to € 180,000 – Spain) or they are related to necessary and verifiable costs (Germany/Thuringia), partly they depend on the degree of citizens' support of the initiative (Germany/i.e. Saxony) as we very well know from the remunerations for parties in general elections. Only occasionally is the successful registration of the initiative enough to be entitled to a proportional remuneration (Germany/Saxony). In the case where the remuneration is related to the (proportional) success of the initiative, at the moment, the state pays between 10 and 30 Eurocents (up to a limited maximum). As far as we know, these remunerations in average cover only between 35% and 50% of the real (initiative-) costs.

European "programs to promote active European citizenship" offer – as mentioned before – substantial financial grants to foster an open, transparent und on-going dialogue with the "organized" civil society. It would therefore be only logical to support trans-European Citizens' Initiatives – which bring citizens of different Member States together to proclaim common trans-European interests – with sufficient financial grants directly. As *Johannes W. Pichler* and I recommended in our book last year, "We Change Europe" (2008), there should be special financial support in several stages: a successfully registered European Citizens' Initiative (by an independent European Initiative Commission) should get first-seed support up to an amount of € 20,000 (or better: € 50,000). In the case of verifiable increasing support by citizens, there should be further grants of € 50,000 – related to a specific ratio formula: e.g. 10,000 citizen declarations in at least two Member States, 50,000 citizens' declarations in at least three Member States, 100,000 citizens' declarations in at least four Member States. The grants have to be used in an orderly (and lawful) manner and should be controlled (on a regular basis and as needed) by the European Initiative Commission.

Philippe D. GROSJEAN

Reflexions and recommendations

Basic beliefs

1) The Salzburg meeting concerns the practice by the participants of their European citizenship and doesn't concern their national citizenship.
2) The resolution to be discussed in Salzburg relates to the implementation of a new democratic right – i.e. the ECI right – that will complement a set of existing rights conferred to citizens and owned by them in virtue of their European citizenship and not their respective national citizenship.
3) European citizens are directly represented at Union level in the European Parliament. Among all the EU institutions, only the Parliament is invested with a legitimacy that is conferred by the direct suffrage of the European citizens.
4) In case European citizens need logistical assistance and/or funding resources in order to concretely exercise a right that they own in virtue of their European citizenship, it is up to the European Parliament to come to their assistance for the simple reason that all other European institutions are elected by the States of the Union and not by the citizens of the Union.

Therefore the proposed Salzburg resolution should be addressed to the European Parliament!

I perfectly understand the difference between the ECI and a petition to the European Parliament. Yet, I am convinced that the resolution should be addressed to the EP – and certainly not to the Commission or the Council – not as a petition but instead on the basis of the Parliament power to request the Commission to submit legislative proposals. (See current Article 192 EC Treaty, future Article 225 FEU Treaty). I know that, during its plenary session in Strasburg on May 6, 2009, the EP will make use of this power, vote on the SYLVIA YVONNE KAUFMANN REPORT and, eventually, approve a formal request to the Commission.

Unfortunately, I am convinced that the above mentioned KAUFMANN REPORT fails on several points to appropriately implement the new ECI right! Therefore, the proposed SALZBURG RESOLUTION should, in my opinion, be amended accordingly.

Basic beliefs (continuation)

5) In democracy, citizens keep their inalienable rights to self-determination and self-government and, consequently, they do not transfer, definitely and irrevocably, power to elected representatives, but merely concede its use and exercise to representatives on condition that the latter report on this use and exercise on an ongoing basis.
6) Therefore democracy demands their participation into the process of using and exercising power and, more particularly, when it relates to the new power conferred to citizens under Article 11.4 TEU-To LISBON.
7) Civil society organizations are the most important channels available to citizens to:
   - Formulate their expectation
   - Inform themselves
   - Debate on arguments and contradictory opinions
   - Deliberate with representatives to whom they conceded the use and exercise of power
   - Evaluate the results from previous decisions and provide feedback
   - Suggest new legislation (ECI)
8) Civil society is therefore inherently legitimate to take part in democracy!
9) EU institutions concocted the expressions: "organized civil society" and "representatives from organized civil society". What do they mean? Within the Permanent Forum, we are very cautious about possible ill-intentions hidden under these expressions.
   a. Do these expressions genuinely relate to the inescapable necessity for European civil society to organize itself in order to be able to play its legitimate role in European democracy?
   b. Or, do they contain a hidden willingness by EU institutions to format and control European civil society in a way that would not endanger nor question their long standing current way of using and exercising power without civil society interfering too much?
10) In the framework of the existing social dialogue – i.e. the dialogue between trades unions, employers' associations and the State – the state authorities do not interfere in the way trades unions and/ or employers' associations organize themselves. Trades unions and employers' associations are mature enough to set their own organization themselves and nominate their "representatives" themselves when it

comes to taking part in a negotiation. Why should it be different in the framework of the legitimate societal dialogue i.e. the dialogue between the authorities and civil society? For which reason are the EU institutions so eager to set rules about civil society representativeness?

11) Civil society organizations (CSO) express a concern that exists in society. They are not speaking on behalf of their constituents the way politicians would do. Often, decision-makers do not distinguish between these two aspects of representation. While politicians' legitimacy has its source in being the delegate or trustee for those living in a specific geographical constituency, there cannot be a similar source of legitimacy for civil society organizations (CSO).

Civil society organizations	**Politicians**
CSO are not due to reach a consensus because it is not their duty to exercise power.	Politicians are due to reach a consensus because it is their duty to use and exercise power.
CSO are due to express the variety of opinions that exist on a given concern.	Politicians are due to examine these opinions, decide upon them and explain their reasons.
CSO are due to evaluate how power is used and exercised.	Politicians are due to report on their use and exercise of power.
CSO are trustee for nobody. They do not have the monopoly of citizens' voices.	Politicians are trustee for people. They have the monopoly of their constituents' voice.

The SYLVIA KAUFMANN REPORT fails on several points

- The Commission being the final addressee of an ECI proposal, it should certainly not be concerned nor allowed to interfere with any one of the stages that precede the formal presentation of the ECI proposal. Indeed the Commission could not be judge in one of its cases!
- The new citizens' right being a European right (see basic belief No 2), one should not allow Member States to get their fingers in the pie! The complete ECI procedure must be carried out without any kind of interference from Member States. If this principle is not firmly respected, one risks causing harm to the genuinely EUROPEAN character of the ECI right. The temptation will be too great for Member States to impede the smooth treatment of an ECI proposal in case they would not like this proposal to reach its final addressee.
- It is obvious from previous attempts concerning the ECI, that European citizens – whatever the way in which civil society succeeds in organizing itself – are to overcome huge logistical, financial, funding and legal difficulties in exercising their new ECI right. European citizens definitely need assistance. This assistance must be provided by

the European Parliament (see basic belief No 4) and not by the Commission.

- As already stated in SYLVIA KAUFMANN REPORT (see item AB), Members of the European Parliament (MEP) are to monitor the process of a citizens' initiative on its political aspects.
- But, in parallel, the EP infrastructure and staff people should also be mobilized because they are European civil servants. As civil servants, they are entrusted with the mission to assist not only the MEP but also the European citizens as they did it already in the two experiments of Citizens' Agora in November 2007 and June 2008. In case the existing EP budget cannot afford the burden of such assistance, it is the European Parliament responsibility to demand additional budget allocations.

- POINT Z: The five stages of the proposed ECI procedure are well identified, except that the fourth one (i.e. statement of its position by the Commission) should become the fifth and final one.
- POINT AE: The question whether Article 11.4 TEU includes – or does not include – initiatives that address Treaty amendments (constitutional citizens' initiatives) IS NOT AT ALL DEBATABLE! Indeed, as the Commission has the power to initiate a proposal to amend the Treaties (see Article 41 TEU), there is no reason why an ECI proposal could not invite the Commission to use this particular power. Civil society should be adamant to strongly support this interpretation because it is the only way offered so far to European citizens to openly and formally express their dissatisfaction with the existing Treaties.

Consequently the proposed Salzburg resolution should be amended!

- It should be addressed to the European Parliament (see above). And, in case that the Parliament adopts, during its plenary session on May 6, 2009, the SYLVIA KAUFMANN REPORT, the Salzburg Resolution should invite the EP to modify it as indicated below.
- The creation of a "guiding, supportive and consulting entity" – THE ECI-AGENCY – is an excellent idea.
- In my opinion this AGENCY should have the following characteristics :
  - It shall be managed and operated jointly by European Parliament's civil servants and members[1] from European Civil society organizations.
  - It shall be responsible for carrying out all the tasks that are listed under the items R to Z in the SYLVIA KAUFMANN REPORT.

1 'Member' is used on purpose instead of 'representatives' because nobody is entitled to be trustee for civil society as a whole!

- It shall be funded partially from the European Parliament's budget and partially from contributions by civil society organizations wanting to initiate an ECI proposal.
- The ECI Agency's staff people shall be composed of:
  - European Parliament's civil servants,
  - Members from CSO designated by those organizations wanting to launch an ECI proposal and only for the duration of time that is necessary to complete the process of their ECI proposal.
- The ECI Agency shall be located in the premises of the European Parliament and have access to its equipment and infrastructure.
- The ECI Agency shall have legal personality, separate from that of the European Parliament.
- The ECI Agency shall be accountable for its action to European civil society organizations and report to them during special sessions of Citizens' Agora.

Amendment: This document is a working document. It has not yet been approved by the Permanent Forum of European Civil Society.

Diana WALLIS

Transcription of the video message for the European Citizens' Initiative Summit in Salzburg

First of all, I am very sorry that I cannot be with you at your conference on the ECI which indeed is a very timely conference. This week here in Strasbourg in the European Parliament we have been discussing a report by a colleague Sylvia Kaufmann that deals particularly with the ECI and how it could be implemented if and when we have the Lisbon Treaty.

What I would like to do is share with you a few thoughts about the ECI and perhaps explain how I have become involved over the years in this issue.

First of all for me, and as I suspect for many other people, the whole idea of instruments like a Citizen's Initiative which is an instrument of direct democracy is linked up with the whole debate about Europe.

In my own case, the first time I ever was able to vote as a young woman was in my own country where we had our first ever national referendum on whether or not we would like to remain in a common European market as it was then called. That was my first experience of a democratic process and I remember absolutely vividly the experience of walking backwards and forwards in the polling station, not sure which way to vote because the politics of my parents meant that I should vote against Europe because they were Socialist, whereas my heart told me that Europe was our future.

But the whole point was that it actually made me think about a political issue and it meant that I could make up my own mind and have my own voice on a political issue rather than electing somebody else to do it for me. And I think that is very important. Particularly in the atmosphere which we live in at the moment in most Western democracies where there are question marks over the whole political process. Certainly in my own country, I am sorry to say, politicians are not held in the highest esteem at the moment.

And therefore I think it is a moment in our political life – as far as possible – to bring the people in, and tools of direct democracy like the ECI are an excellent way of doing that.

If perhaps I can put it in another manner: we have always been used to a model of democracy that involves electing people to make decisions for us. But if we think about it, that form of democracy comes from the age of the horse and carriage, from a very slow age where you would elect people from all over the country We are given modern means of communication and other things that has to be a better way of doing our politics and would involve everybody much more in decision-making.

Now there are also attempts to use petitions. But petitions are a very negative instrument. Here in the European Parliament we have had for many years a very active petitions committee and it provides a wonderful formal process for citizens to complain or bring to our attention European law that is not working on their behalf. That is excellent and it often results in a process being taken by the Commission to make sure that European law is implemented properly and sometimes indeed it results in proposals in longer terms for legislation. But it is essentially a negative instrument. It is about complaining and I think what most of us wanted to see was a positive instrument, indeed a way in which European citizens and anybody – if they so wished – could become involved in sort of pushing the legislative button in persuading the European institutions that here was an issue upon which a European law should be made.

And so when we had the Convention – it now seems years ago – there was this whole movement towards developing a form of Citizens Initiative on the European level. And we saw that text eventually find its way to the Draft Constitution and it is still there in the Lisbon Treaty, which is why we have been looking upon possible implementing rules. The point is: basically it would give the chance to a million citizens across Europe to launch a process to get a European law into European legislation. It is fundamentally something that is a request to the Commission.

But the text in the Treaty is very simple; it doesn't give any of the technical details how this would be other than a million signatures. Therefore we have to decide – in terms of signatures – should they come from a certain number of member states? The answer seems to be at least a quarter. That would work with certain other requirements within the treaties.

How do you go about gathering the signatures? Should there be a test before you start? Perhaps there should be some sort of test at the beginning because what we don't want to do is raise expectations rather like happened with the petition for the so-called 'one seat' for the European Parliament. Over a million people signed the petition but unfortunately the Commission could do nothing about that issue. So it tends to result in disappointment. So better probably that in the first instance we make sure that this is something where the European Community cannot and the European Commission can bring forward a legislative proposal.

So there will be a lot of issues to think about and particularly how our Parliament should be involved in this process. Obviously there are many that feel this could pre-empt the Parliament's rights. I believe it should be a matter of Parliament and citizens working together and that you could see parliamentarians championing initiatives. But we shouldn't get in the way – we should work together with our citizens!

It seems to me that the ECI has the chance to make Europe far more democratic than many member states are, particularly my own. It would be impossible to envisage such a system at the moment in the United Kingdom. The only petitions we have are ones on the 10, Downing Street website and they go nowhere and they feed frustration and annoyance with the political process. What I want to see is an instrument that works at a European level and allows our citizens to tell us what they would like to see on the European statute book and for us to be able to work with them in the Parliament to make that a reality.

Jo LEINEN

Transcript of the video message for the European Citizens' Initiative Summit in Salzburg

I send my best wishes to all participants of the European Citizens' Summit in Salzburg and also would like to thank the hosts for organizing such an important conference. I hope that you will have participants from many countries of the European Union as well as from Switzerland, who has the most experience in this field.

I am delivering this message from Strasbourg and from the last plenary session of the European Parliament in this legislature. As chair of the Constitutional Committee, I am especially delighted that we have just now adopted with a large majority the report of Mrs. Sylvia-Yvonne Kaufmann about the European Citizens' Initiative.

The Lisbon Treaty – the reform treaty of the European Union – has a general orientation: the concept of a participative democracy. No Europe of elites, no Europe of only governments and states, but a Europe of citizens. We are taking a big leap towards this goal with the new treaty. However, we still have a long way to go. The Lisbon treaty is one step and I think it is an important one in the history of European integration. But it does not yet meet the goal of a United States of Europe with a fully-fledged democratic infrastructure.

The European Citizens' Initiative is a new tool. I am pleased that this idea of the Convention for the European Constitution can now be implemented. The idea that with one million signatures from a relevant number of countries, citizens can put an issue on the political agenda of the European institutions in Brussels is great progress. I believe that this will become a dynamic tool for the creation of a European public and also for bringing together people with a common concern or request from Portugal to Poland, from all 27 Member States, from this greatly expanded European Union.

With the Kaufmann Report, the Parliament has been a precursor and we hope that once the new European Commission is constituted, it will make use of its initiative right and put forward a proposition for legislation on this matter. We need legally established conditions for the European

Citizens' Initiative and we demand that this does not become a "make believe instrument". The European Citizens' Initiative is a serious, constitutionally laid down instrument of the people to allow them to directly intervene in European politics. The European Parliament will make sure that the initiatives put forward by the citizens do not disappear in the downs of bureaucracy but that they are duly processed and answered, ideally with a successful legislative proposition or a program that the citizens of Europe expect.

The European Citizens' Initiative is only one instrument for participatory democracy. I know that the debate goes much further, for example if we also need European referenda. And I really do mean European referenda. With now 27 and soon even more Member States, I am not a supporter of a cascade of national popular votes. These would be a dead end. Our experience shows us that national referenda are determined by controversies in domestic policies and that the European Union is taken hostage for particular issues or for problems which a Member State or even just one political party in that Member State might have with itself. This cannot be the solution. I believe that for the next steps of the European integration, we need to discuss the possibility of a European referendum; a vote on the same day and in all Member States, with a qualified majority rule. The Lisbon Treaty provides the double majority rule for the votes in the Council. I could imagine a qualified majority for the European referendum to ensure that smaller Member States are sufficiently legitimated and that these popular votes are not dominated by few big countries.

I also would like to mention the civil dialogue as a tool that is introduced by the Lisbon Treaty. We already have the social dialogue with social partners. Now, we will also use the civil dialogue together with the organised civil society and the non-governmental organisations. This will be extremely important. As a single person, a citizen is often powerless, but citizens can be very powerful when they are part of an organisation. Amnesty International or Greenpeace only are examples. The European institutions need to be in constant dialogue with civil society, bringing the project of European integration closer to the citizens again. In the Parliament, we have started a series of events under the name "AGORA" that has evolved to a successful tool for exchanging ideas with civil society actors. This instrument will surely be developed further in the future.

We can see that there have been a number of steps forward for the Citizenship of the Union. I wish the Citizens' Summit in Salzburg a good success. The newly elected Citizens' Chamber – the newly elected European Parliament – will thankfully pick up the suggestions from Salzburg and work with these ideas in the next legislature.

Goodbye and see you somewhere in Europe. Jo Leinen

Joe MATHEWS

California's Troubles, Europe's Future – and the need for a more direct Representative Democracy

Few Californians are aware of the European Citizen's initiative. They should be. California is struggling to figure out how to fix its direct democracy, a major culprit in its budget troubles. Europeans are launching a debate on how best to structure the process for their own continent-wide initiative. In their search for best practices, Europe and California are on parallel tracks.

To be sure, Europe's citizen initiative and California's ballot initiative are hardly the same. But both places share a common concern: the problems of scale. In California, a nation-state of more than 38 million people spread over 424,000 square kilometers, the constitution requires the gathering of hundreds of thousands of signatures to qualify an initiative for the ballot. Given the fact that only three in four signatures collected are valid, the number of signatures that must be gathered for each initiative is one million – the exact same number envisioned by the Lisbon Treaty for the new citizen's initiative.

The hard, logistical fact is that the gathering of so many signatures over a great geographic space requires considerable money and organization. In California, obtaining the signatures requires the employment of professional petition circulators, who are paid $2 per signature and more. This high cost reflects more than the scale of the project, however. Complying with the restrictions and regulations of the process is a costly endeavor. As the European Commission's own green paper on the citizen's initiative notes, "Whilst a high threshold would indeed ensure that the initiative is sufficiently representative, it would nevertheless make the procedure more burdensome. On the other hand a low threshold would render the initiative more accessible, but less representative." California faces the same quandary. In the U.S. constitutional system, where courts have made clear that rights of free expression include the right to donate as one wishes to political causes, the high cost of qualifying initiatives has largely limited the process to wealthy individuals and interest groups.

The following paper offers an account of the California initiative process and solutions for addressing its peculiar deficiencies. The lessons of California, for direct democracy professionals in Europe and elsewhere, have little to do with the specifics of distribution requirements or initiative registration. California's failures show the necessity of flexible systems of initiative and referendum that are integrated with the legislative and executive institutions of government. Because California does not have such an integrated system, our proud state stands on the brink.

Here is the story about how California could meet this challenge. It starts one year ago.

Darrell Steinberg had to decide whether to betray himself.

In February 2009, Steinberg led the California State Senate as its president pro tem. But he was locked in negotiations that made him feel like a hostage. The country's economic recession had caused a historic collapse in state tax revenues. California faced a budget deficit in the tens of millions. The state had no cash in its main accounts and had already raided hundreds of special funds scattered around the treasury to pay its bills. The world's credit markets were so damaged that the borrowing short-term cash was prohibitively expensive. By late February, California would be out of cash. The state controller was preparing to pay bills with IOUs.

Steinberg desperately wanted to balance the budget. But every political option was blocked, many of them by previous citizen's ballot initiatives. The Democratic majority was willing to raise taxes, but the minority Republicans, using the leverage of voter-approved requirement of a two-thirds vote to raise taxes, were balking. As negotiators searched for money, Republicans suggested diverting tax dollars from two popular programs, early childhood services and mental health. These programs were rare birds. Each was established by a ballot initiative (Prop 10 in 1998 for early childhood; Prop 63 in 2004 for mental health). And neither was the sort of "something for nothing" measure – a spending mandate without dedicated funds – so common to the California ballot. To the contrary, each initiative had identified a new, dedicated source of tax revenue (tobacco taxes for early childhood; an income tax surcharge on millionaires for mental health) to fund its programs. Having been established by voters, each program existed outside the normal budget process. And because they were running a big surplus, they were tempting targets for lawmakers short on cash. In negotiations, legislative leaders debated taking roughly half of those surpluses: $1.6 billion over five years from early childhood and more than $500 million over two years from mental health.

This was dangerous territory for Steinberg personally. Not only were such programs a top priority for his party and its donor base, but Steinberg himself had been the author of Prop 63, the initiative that established the tax for mental health. Unable to get such a tax through the Assembly when he chaired the budget committee there, the legislator had, like any interest group, taken his case to the people, and scored a victory. Prop 63 was the signature achievement of his career. It had given him statewide notoriety, and was one reason why he was leading the state Senate.

Steinberg thus faced the choice: do his job or undo his record. The Republican legislative leaders were willing to put up enough votes for a budget that included temporary tax increases. This act of GOP responsibility was also a political risk, a violation of anti-tax orthodoxy in a party that had grown smaller and more conservative. As part of their price for the tax increase, the Republicans demanded Steinberg take his own risk. Steinberg also saw that if he didn't go along, the outcome would be perverse: the state would be cutting basic health programs even as it allowed these two initiative-protected programs to maintain surpluses. Reluctantly, he agreed to take money from his own program, as well as from early childhood.

"We were faced with a $41 billion deficit and a political system where it's next to impossible to raise taxes through the legislative process," Steinberg would later say. "But I had a different responsibility, a responsibility as leader in the legislature to set an example. As we were asking others, including Republicans, to violate their own orthodoxy, I couldn't say you can look at everything except what's important to me. I didn't like it, but I had to support it."[1]

A deal was reached, but that wasn't the end of the story. In every other state in the union, the legislative agreement to take the funds would have closed the matter. In California, that was not enough. Steinberg might be the leader of the majority in the upper house of the legislature. He might be the author of the program he had reluctantly agreed to raid. An initiative simply couldn't be changed by elected leaders or its author, only by another vote of the people. The initiative process existed in a world all its own, beyond checks and balances. So the best the legislature could do was draw up two ballot measures – Propositions 1D and Proposition 1E – to get voter approval before the money could be used to balance the budget.

It wasn't enough for Steinberg to betray himself; he'd have to get permission first.

In May 2009, Californians would cast ballots on Propositions 1D and 1E – plus four other compromise measures that came out of the same desperate negotiations to change the budget before the state ran out of cash. The six measures did not exist because a majority of legislators wanted them on the ballot. To the contrary, lawmakers would have been happy to enact the deal themselves without having to ask voters. The measures were all there because California's system had forced lawmakers' hands.

1 Darrell Steinberg interview, April 9, 2009.

Prop 1A was a compromise, forced upon the Democratic majority by the handful of Republicans who agreed to vote for the deal and reach the two-thirds threshold, to raise taxes temporarily in exchange for establishment of a rainy day fund. Prop 1F, a populist measure to tie legislative pay to budget timing, was another Republican demand enacted only because of the two-thirds leverage. Prop 1B resulted from a deal with the teachers unions, using the leverage that an earlier citizen's initiative on education provided them, that permitted short-term budget cuts in exchange for a change in funding formulas to boost education spending over the long term. Prop 1C, which sought to borrow against future lottery proceeds, had to go on the ballot because it altered the 1984 ballot initiative that created the lottery.

Voters were themselves responsible for the existence of these ballot measures, but Californians went to the polls grudgingly, blaming the legislature for sticking them with the responsibility of choosing. Surveys showed that significant blocs of voters – one-third of those surveyed by Field in April 2009 and 50 percent of Republicans in the poll – were opposing all measures on the ballot at least in part because they thought the legislature shouldn't have been bothering voters with these questions – despite the constitutional requirement that voters be bothered.

This mood prevailed. Five of the six measures were defeated, with only Prop 1F, the populist blast at legislative pay, winning.

The failed special election was one more casualty of the cycle of contempt produced by the initiative process. The public distrusts the legislature and their elected officials. So voters, preferring to trust themselves, make major policy decisions via ballot initiative. These decisions, because of the requirement that initiatives not be changed by legislators alone, further tie the hands of lawmakers. The frustrated lawmakers find it difficult to solve pressing problems, further fueling the public frustration that produces more initiatives and more hand-tying. This vicious cycle produces anger, ballot box budgeting, and poor governance.

This system also defies accountability. Who is really responsible for the problems of lawmaking and budgeting in California? Lawmakers, with good reason, can blame the voters who have reduced their ability to come up with solutions. Voters, with good reason, can blame the lawmakers, who after all have high-paying jobs and plenty of time to balance budgets but never seem able to do so.

The question is debated endlessly. The fact that there is no clear answer is precisely the problem. The legislature and the voters each legislate. They are part of the same branch of government. But these two halves of the branch are not linked together in any meaningful way. California's system puts lawmakers and voters on entirely separate tracks – even though they are shaping the same laws and the same constitution. The legislative branch is unaccountable precisely because it is divided in this way.

There is no data to suggest that our legislators are lesser beings than those who haunt statehouses and Congresses and Parliament the world over. And California is not the only place with direct democracy. Twenty-four states have some form of initiative at the state level. All fifty states offer direct democracy at the local level. And more than a hundred of the world's countries permit direct democracy at the state or local level.[2] Switzerland, the only country with a federal system of direct democracy (a system that inspired the Progressives who adopted initiative and referendum in California), is among the world's best governed, least corrupt, and most peaceful nations.

What makes California different? It's the design of the state's system of direct democracy, and in particular, its initiative process.

Specifically, California has the most powerful – and thus the most inflexible – initiative in the world. The legislature has no constitutional power to stop an initiative from reaching the ballot. Nor does the governor or any member of the executive branch. Judicial authorities can block initiatives with constitutional infirmities, but precedent sets a high standard for doing so. In all twenty-three other states with the initiative process, legislatures may change a law enacted by initiative. Sometimes, there is a brief waiting period before lawmakers can act – two years – or maybe a super-majority is required to make a change. California is the only place in the world where a statute enacted by initiative can only be undone with another popular vote (unless the original initiative permits legislative amendment).[3]

Initiatives to amend the constitution present a similar problem. An initiative constitutional amendment requires only a simple majority of voters to pass. But to amend or revise the constitution, the legislature must muster a two-thirds vote – and the approval of the voters.

These incentives give California's direct democracy the strongest pro-initiative bias of any such system in the world. The other tools of direct democracy have fallen into disuse. The recall is uncommon; the 2003 recall of Gov Gray Davis was the first and only recall of a statewide elected official. The referendum is rarely used – fewer than seventy have been filed in a near century of California direct democracy, and only fifty have qualified for the ballot.[4] By contrast, more than a hundred ballot initiatives a year are now filed with the state attorney general's office. This

2 Bruno Kaufmann. Address to Global Forum on Modern Direct Democracy, Aarau, Switzerland, October 1, 2008.

3 Democracy by Initiative: Shaping California's Fourth Branch of Government, 10. David Altman, Address to the Global Forum on Modern Direct Democracy in Aarau, Switzerland, October 1, 2008. In recent years, more initiative sponsors in California have included language permitting legislative amendments of statutory initiatives, usually via supermajorities. Between 1990 and 2006, 33 of the 42 initiative statutes to qualify for the ballot permitted some form of amendment.

4 California Secretary of State records, including this list of referenda at http://www.sos.ca.gov/elections/referenda.htm.

makes sense. Why bother with a referendum (reversing a law of the legislature) or a recall of a legislator when an initiative permits you to write a law or constitutional amendment that the legislature will never be able to change on its own?

Such an inflexible system has many consequences. Budget priorities can be locked in easily, and they persist even when revenues diminish or when the priorities of a majority of Californians change. Civil rights may be taken away by the slimmest of majorities in the California system, while revising those restrictions often requires legislative super-majorities. Effectively, voters can set in cement laws and constitutional amendments that will govern the state long after they are dead or moved away, even if new majorities would like something different.

Such a direct democracy isn't worthy of the name. It isn't very direct. And it sure isn't democratic. Put simply, initiatives provide voters not with direct engagement with their government, but with a way to circumvent their state government and frustrate future majorities.

Since the 1911 special election that gave California its strange direct democracy, reformers have been trying to fix its defects. There is no shortage of ideas.

Restrictions on the process. Since 1920, when the legislature tried and failed to eliminate the initiative and referendum, state elites have been trying to impose limits on initiatives. Some reforms would limit the issues subject to initiative. Others would raise the number of signatures required to qualify an initiative.

Removing money from the process. In California, good government groups have sought to impose limits on donations to initiative campaigns. They also have sought to ban or put restrictions on paid petition circulators, who do the overwhelming majority of signature gathering on initiative petitions.

Open up the process. Among the suggestions are to eliminate time limits for signature gathering, thus giving volunteer petition circulators plenty of time to collect the hundreds of thousands of signatures required for the ballot. In recent years, there have been efforts to permit signature gathering and petition circulation over the Internet.

Providing better information. A recent report by the Center for Governmental Studies and a 2002 state commission each recommended upgrades to the information the state provides to voters about initiatives. CGS urged that restrictions be adopted on the lengths of measures – roughly a third of initiatives in the past decade have been more than 5,000 words, too long and too confusing for many voters.

Each of these approaches, particularly those requiring more information for voters, have merit and could improve the process slightly. But they all have drawbacks. Imposing new restrictions on the process could add to the costs of qualifying measures and running campaigns, thus making the initiative process even more of a rich person's game.

Many of the ideas for removing money from the process have been tried and struck down by federal and state courts as unconstitutional restrictions on political expression. On the other side, opening up the process and making the sponsorship of initiatives cheaper might produce more initiatives – and in California's system, that means more whips and chains that restrict the ability of elected leaders to govern effectively.

The big problem with these reforms is more fundamental. None of them address the divide in California's legislative branch, the inflexibility of the initiative process, and the problems of accountability that result.

Reckoning with these structural challenges requires a full redesign not only of the initiative process but also of the relationship between the legislature and direct democracy. Lawmakers and voters are now at odds, with each half of the legislative branch frustrated and hamstrung by the other. That divide must be bridged, so that the legislature better serves direct democracy, and direct democracy better serves the legislature.

Legislative reform and initiative reform can't be considered separately. They are two sides of the same coin. Lawmakers and voters should be partners in lawmaking – not antagonists who are free to work around each other. This requires two related sets of reforms. Not only must the initiative system be redesigned to bring the legislature into the process, as many commentators suggest. The legislature must also be changed to bring the voters into the process.

Successful reform in this area should not restrict voters or lawmakers. It should seek to free them, and give them more power and discretion – in ways that allow them to engage in constructive conversation with each other.

The goal is nothing less than a more direct and more democratic direct democracy. Lawmakers must have more ability to balance priorities, budget, and legislate as best they see fit. At the same time, voters need to have greater freedom to pass judgment on the products of this greater legislative freedom. Ideally, the two sides of the legislative branch could be integrated in a way that allows the legislature and voters to do what they do best. The legislature, using its time and staff and expertise, should have the unquestioned authority to legislate. Voters must have unquestioned authority to check the legislature, sending back laws and budgets they do not like for more work.

Fashioning reform requires reckoning with a hard political fact. Any new limits on the initiative process are poisonous. Yes, surveys show widespread public dissatisfaction with aspects of the process. Surveys consistently show that more than three in four California voters support retaining the process. Abolition is not an option, nor should it be. A well-designed system of initiative and referendum would provide a useful check on representative government.

What would such a system look like?

Initiatives, as proposed laws and constitutional amendments, must adhere to the same rules as legislation. Initiative proponents would submit their language to nonpartisan staffers inside the Capitol – at the legislative counsel's office, which would produce the actual legislative language of any measure that circulates. This would tend to prevent drafting errors and unintended consequences, and produce clearer initiatives.

Most importantly, initiatives would no longer be immune from legislative amendment. Any initiative that passes would be subject to amendment or elimination by the legislature. There should no longer be two classes of laws – one passed by the legislature and subject to amendment, one passed by the voters and essentially protected from amendment.

Such a change would put California in line with its neighbors. Every other state permits legislative changes to initiatives, either through a majority vote, a supermajority vote or by majority vote after a waiting period. As a compromise, lawmakers might have to wait for one legislative session – two years – after an initiative passes, out of respect for the will of the voters.

This is not a radical change. Responsible initiative sponsors in California have often included provisions permitting the legislature to make amendments. Thirty-three out of the forty-two initiatives approved by voters between 1990 and 2006 included some provision permitting legislative change.[5] And Prop 9, the 1974 Political Reform Act – which was one of the first initiatives to include language permitting legislative amendment without a vote of the people – has been amended more than two hundred times.

Establish higher standards for constitutional amendments that give voters and lawmakers complimentary powers to add to or subtract from the document. Currently, an amendment may be added with a simple majority vote of the people. But the constitution cannot be amended by the legislature, or substantially revised, without a two-thirds vote and another vote of the people. This dynamic – making it harder to add than to edit or revise the document – is one reason why California's constitution has grown so long.

To reverse that trend, new rules should make it more difficult to add to the constitution – and easier to revise it or edit things out. Voters and lawmakers should have similar powers in this area, along two tracks.

The first track would permit the constitution to be amended or revised by a majority vote of the people – or a majority vote of the legislature, followed by a vote of the people – but only if the proposal showed sustained support over two election cycles. In the case of an amendment or revision offered via initiative, the proposed change would have to win a majority vote in two consecutive elections. If the legislature is the body introducing the change, the amendment or revision would have to win

5 Democracy by Initiative: Shaping California's Fourth Branch of Government, 10.

majority votes in two consecutive legislative sessions, with the people also approving by majority vote.

If faster constitutional action is required, a second track would permit quick passage but with a higher voting standard. To alter the constitution in just one cycle, two-thirds of voters would have to approve in the case of the initiative, or two-thirds of the legislature (followed by a vote of the people) if lawmakers offer the change.

Any initiative that would impose supermajority requirements must pass by the same supermajority to take effect. For example, if a measure were to require a 60 percent vote of the legislature to raise taxes, the measure itself would have to receive 60 percent support at the polls. This would be an important check on supermajorities; Prop 13, which included the current two-thirds requirement for tax increases, was approved in 1978 with a big majority but with less than two-thirds of the vote.

Make all ballot initiatives and bond measures live within the legislative budget. To control the epidemic of something for nothing, every spending measure placed before voters needs to pay for itself, either with new revenue or offsetting spending cuts.

Permit the legislature to enact each initiative or place a counter-proposal next to the initiative on the ballot.

Under the current system, the legislature holds hearings on each initiative, but there is no formal mechanism for negotiations between initiative sponsors and lawmakers. There should be. Sponsors who qualify an initiative should be guaranteed an up or down vote on the measure. In addition, lawmakers should be able to offer amendments that the initiative sponsor may accept or reject.

If the initiative sponsor decides to take the measure to the ballot anyway, the legislature should have the right to place a counter-proposal on the ballot, on the very same page as the initiative, via majority vote. Currently, lawmakers sometimes put a measure elsewhere on the ballot that is meant to counter an initiative, but not on the same page and only with a two-thirds vote. As a result, it is often unclear to voters that they are reckoning with two competing proposals, one from the legislature and the other from an initiative sponsor).

Most countries that permit citizen's initiatives offer legislative counter-proposals. Switzerland, which inspired California's direct democracy, requires just such a counter-proposal for every initiative. Sometimes, the counter-proposal is constructive and seeks to meet the sponsor's goal by a different method. Sometimes, the counter-proposal is a harsh rebuttal by the legislature. Whatever the case, Swiss ballots place a third question next to the initiative and the counter-proposal: If both measures were to win, which would you prefer? This permits voters who support the goal of both the initiative and the counter-proposal to express a preference. This third question also permits voters who oppose a concept to choose the measure that they see as less threatening.

California should adopt this three-question set up – initiative, counter-proposal, and preference between the two – not only because it provides more influence for lawmakers but also because it provides considerably more choice and power for voters. Under the current system, voters have a simple, binary choice on initiatives: yes or no. Under the three-question system, voters have eight voting options on one question, instead of just the two permitted under the current system. Consider:

1. Yes on initiative, yes on counter, prefer initiative if both pass
2. Yes on initiative, yes on counter, prefer counter if both pass
3. Yes on initiative, no on counter, prefer initiative if both pass
4. Yes on initiative, no on counter, prefer counter (an unlikely result obviously)
5. No on initiative, yes on counter, prefer initiative (unlikely)
6. No on initiative, yes on counter, prefer counter if both pass
7. No on initiative, no on counter, prefer initiative if both pass
8. No on initiative, no on counter, prefer counter if both pass

In a three-question initiative system, campaigns would produce more informed voters. How? Under the current system, voters must consider the initiative in isolation, without any point of comparison. Feelings about the issue often drive debate, and the details of the measure get little scrutiny. But in a three-question system, a campaign is likely to be comparative, focusing attention and debate on the contents of the two measures. The central question of such a race would be: what's different between these two measures? Such comparative campaigns would produce scrutiny of the legislative details, and help voters make more informed choices. Information is power.

Make it easier for voters to overturn the legislature through a more referendum-based direct democracy.

Reform to the initiative process must enhance lawmakers' power by ensuring that the legislature is the undisputed headquarters of writing and drafting new laws. By retaining the power to amend initiatives, legislators would find no part of the law off-limits.

But voters need additional power to check the legislature. That power could be found in an oft-neglected tool of California's direct democracy: the referendum.

A referendum is a ballot measure that does not propose a law – but instead permits voters to block an act of the legislature. The California state constitution, as we have seen, is biased in favor of the initiative. It is just as easy to qualify initiative, in terms of signatures, as it is to qualify a referendum. And it is usually less expensive to qualify an initiative, because the time limit for qualifying an initiative is two months longer – 150 days – than the 90-day limit for referenda. Signature gatherers can charge ballot measures sponsors more money for signatures when they know time is short.

In addition, the constitution makes it possible for initiatives to be introduced on almost any subject matter. The referendum power, however, is limited, to certain legislative subjects and to measures passed in the normal course of business. Tax and appropriation bills and legislation passed under "urgency," or emergency, provisions are exempt from referendum. As a result, fewer than seventy-five referenda have filed for the ballot in California since 1911. In the same century, more than 1,100 initiatives have been filed and more than 300 have qualified for the ballot. This initiative-centered direct democracy is unique to California and other western states. In the rest of the world, the referendum, or reversal of legislative action, not the initiative, is by far the most common type of ballot measure.

To balance the enhanced power of lawmakers to amend initiatives, voters need more power to block them via referendum. This could be accomplished in several ways. The signature gathering standards for a referendum might be lowered substantially, perhaps to 1 percent of the number of votes cast in the most recent gubernatorial election. With such a standard, enough signatures to qualify a referendum could be gathered in a matter of weeks. Under a system that provides for quick referenda, urgency and some tax and spending bills could be made subject to voter reversals as well.

Such a reform would not reduce the number of ballot measures or the ability of the people to decide big questions. If anything, it might give people more measures and more choices. But the goal would be to make most California ballot measures referenda – verdicts on the product of the legislature – instead of initiatives. In short, California's direct democratic system would be referendum-based, not initiative-based.

Such a system, by its very nature, would be more integrated with the legislative process. When Californians vote on initiatives now, they are voting on proposed laws and amendments that have not been vetted in the legislature. This may be democracy, but it is not a direct judgment on the government. It is an end run around that government. When they vote on referenda, they are passing judgment on the legislature. That is direct communication between the people and their elected officials.

How might such a system work in practice? Ideally, lawmakers and voters would be partners, with the legislature making suggestions and the public saying yea or nay. It is likely that controversial legislation would be presented to the people multiple times before it wins approval. This process would not be without rancor. But it would channel that rancor into democratic verdicts, as voters and lawmakers bat proposals back and forth until consensus emerges.

This system would offer more power and choice to voters. It also would provide more power and autonomy for elected representatives in legislation. And there would be more direct interplay between voters and legislators, via counter proposals and more frequent referenda.

Legislators would be more accountable for their work, since, under a referendum-based system, they frequently would have to convince voters to accept their deals and compromises. Much of the money and scrutiny that initiatives currently attract would be redirected to the legislature, the source of referenda upon which voters would pass judgment. Voters would have to pay more attention to the legislature; they'd be voting not on initiative abstractions but on legislative deals, with all their trade-offs.

With these reforms, California's system of initiative and referendum would be worthy of the name, direct democracy.

Walter CUDLIP

Transcript of the video message for the European Citizens' Initiative Summit in Salzburg

Hello, my name is Walter Cudlip and I live in Australia. My colleagues Charles Rye from Bermuda and Wendy Lotan from Canada are producing a documentary series about democracy.

We each live in countries that call themselves democratic. But our system of representative government was really designed for the great benefit of one particular segment of the society. Our populations have the right to vote and that right makes them think that they can control the government.

Unfortunately the political system in our countries only gives us the ability to give our powers away at election time. We've been persuaded that this is the best way for most people to enjoy a happy and prosperous life. We are also persuaded that it is better to let the professionals do the work of making the decisions. We are not educated enough, not interested enough or we don't have enough time to do this complicated and sophisticated work. And most of us think this is true. We are too busy just going to work, raising our families and living our lives to get involved with governance.

We may not be too happy with all the things our government does and even we grudge the taxes we have to pay which seem to benefit others more than ourselves. But this seems to be the way it is and there's not much we can do than vote out the people we don't like and vote in somebody else.

Then along come crises like the current financial mess and then the climate changes the situation. Suddenly our jobs disappear, our pensions shrink and all the hard work we did and all the decisions we made are swept away by forces beyond our control and after our own borders. We are faced with the cold, hard truth that we need more say in the policies our governments create and the realization that our systems actually prevent us from being knowledgeable about what constitutes good policy.

Knowing that our governments are not providing the best results is one thing. Finding an alternative is quite another.

What system is there, that doesn't dispense with the benefits we enjoy but gives us more control of our politicians? Our discovery is that most people who have inherited some form of the Westminster system are ignorant of any other form of democracy. We feel powerless but don't know where to turn for answers.

True to the old maxime – if you want to hide something, put it in plain sight – the best example of how to reform government truly democratically and how to give the people sovereignty has been sitting there for a long time: Switzerland has over a century of experience with direct democracy instruments. Other European citizens have started to introduce a new form of modern direct democracy as well.

Yet it remains an untapped resource for the rest of us across the world. As documentary film makers we can see the issue clearly before us and we can see why we need to share it with our fellow citizens.

Direct democracy as practiced in Switzerland and some other European countries is a system with tools for citizens to actively make or amend laws, to remain at the heart of the government and take responsibility for the society.

Citizens in our countries and many others don't have this freedom – and we should! The documentary series we are producing aims to inform and mobilize our population to change by illustrating how democratic government emerged from the 18th and 19th century within free market economies, how business, political parties, unions and corporate interests have taken control of government to the exclusion of the citizens and what can be done to change the status quo.

We intend to offer the people a view of what it could look like if direct democracy and citizens' initiatives were the cornerstones of a new system of governing. Therefore we welcome very much any move on the European level to introduce forms of direct democracy as well. By establishing a European agenda setting, too for the citizens, it would make a substantial difference and if this new tool is supplemented with a supportive infrastructure, this difference will become even bigger. It would serve as a guidepost to other territories to implement beneficial change!

Andreas GROSS

The European Citizens' Initiative can become more than it would seem to be today

A comparison based upon the Zurich history of Direct Democracy in the 19th century

The character of the new European Citizens' Initiative Right (ECI) is very controversial at any rate. There are those who emphasize strongly that it represents the first transnational, participative citizen right in the world. Until now, Europeans had nothing to say with the exception of the European Parliament elections. In similar ways, until now, direct democracy was restricted to individual National States. The ECI is consequently a pioneer work for the European Union (EU) as well as for democracy.

The fact that the ECI has survived the confusion of the mangled treaty revisions of the 2000 decade unscathed can be interpreted as the expression of the opinion of many that the EU has just as much need of direct-democratic structural elements as democracy a transnational structural level. This is because, with careful arrangement and contextualizing of its processes, direct democracy provides just what the EU most urgently needs today: more direct legitimacy with the citizens, stronger bonds between the EU and its citizens, identification options, but also more civil societal integration powers, a European public as well as more transnational, European reflections and deliberations.

Democracy, direct as well as indirect, must stand on its own feet for the sake of its own substantial promise but also finally at the transnational level. If not, it will succeed at neither bridling nor civilizing the long-since transnational market powers in the interest of most individuals and the environment. It is rather the case today that the interests of the most powerful market actors dictate to the National States which necessary steps they are to take in their own economic interest – as the case may be, even against the will of the majority of affected citizens. Freedom, however, like the primacy of politics, means the opposite. In order for deference to be paid to the democratically-achieved will of the majority of people, this democratic formation of will must happen transnationally and will, with this special legitimation, also be better enforceable.

On the other hand, many of those Europeans who are well-acquainted with the idiosyncrasies of direct democracy[1] emphasize just as rightly that the ECI, despite the term it carries of initiative, cannot be compared to one of the public initiatives common to Switzerland This is because in Swiss terminology, an initiative enables the passing of referendums against any resistance whatsoever by governmental or parliamentary majorities as long as a sufficient number of signatures were collected within a legally prescribed deadline. The enormous strength of direct democracy rests precisely upon this right of a few committed people to impose the discussion of an unpopular question upon the whole society, should it avoid this discussion.

In comparison to a Swiss popular initiative, which is described as a popular referendum in Germany, the ECI in the Swiss concept of direct democracy is indeed "only" a public right of motion, like what exists at canton level for example in the cantons of Solothurn and Nidwalden. Thus, in Switzerland as well, a plebiscite, called binding referendum (Volksentscheid) in Germany, cannot be enforced. A public motion is simply the right of a very small group of citizens to be allowed to present an appropriate proposition to Parliament, or the authority with competence for legislative initiatives.

The person who reduces the ECI to a public motion along Swiss lines or who even thinks that this is nothing more than a heftier petition makes a double mistake. Firstly, he or she errs in the addressee. A petition is directed to the European Parliament within the EU, the ECI to the Commission. Secondly, more importantly, he or she misjudges the fact that in the EU, also the indirect, in other words, parliamentarian democracy is not (yet) as developed as we would expect in a traditional federalist federal state. However, in its democracy form, the EU actually resembles more a confederation and not a federal state. A confederation, however, whose center has taken on an enormous capacity for legislature enforcement, without this being – regardless of "Lisbon" – sufficiently democratically substantiated. Because what we should not forget: neither does the EP have the legislative initiative at its disposal like a "normal" parliament; rather, the commission may, as the sole body that can initiate acts of legislature, only make appropriate proposals. Thus, by supporting the ECI in the past, the EP showed itself prepared to share its proposal right of legislation revision for the attention of the Commission, or more precisely that of its majority, with a million of Europeans. That is not bad, especially when we recall how reluctantly if not defensively politicians normally treat citizens rights, or, as the case may be, how rarely they are prepared to

1 A prime example of these voices might be the well-known Valais EU skeptic from Switzerland, Paul Ruppen (Brig). He is the editor of the very critical, national-economic Europe Magazine and describes the ECI in a letter to the editor as little more than a petition right. ("Sonntagszeitung" on 31.10.09)

normally share their power with citizens, especially when it itself is only limited. Regardless of the fact that the sharing of power with citizens is the sole source of any legitimate political power in a democracy in any case, and one of the fundamental principles of the philosophy of direct democracy.

Thus, the person emphasizing the ECI's limited range and power of implementation is correct. It is, in common language usage, nothing more than an "agenda initiative", a possibility for citizens to bring an idea to the order of business of the body which has competence for legislative initiatives. Regardless, this is not negligible within today's structures of European democracy. Since not even the EP majority has more legislative initiative power than this!

Emphasizing this relativity of the ECI is actually quite important at the moment. Due to the fact that in these weeks, the EU Commission will decide on the legal arrangement of the ECI's usage. The hurdles, like the signatures required and from how many countries a relevant amount of citizen signatures have to sign should not be set too high. Because of the fact that these people may not offer more than a suggestion, stimulus for discussion.

Regardless, we may not leave the relativizing of the ECI as is. Because in the history of democracy, there were other humble beginnings.

This was the case in the canton of Zurich which experienced a revolution which was actually democratic in the winter of 1867/1868 which resulted in the first direct-democratic constitution world-wide in April 1869. The decisive lever which made it possible for the powerful democratic movement in December 1867 to completely pry away the regime which underestimated the economic, social misery was an instrument which exactly this government had itself introduced a few years prior and of which it then thought "it is of almost no practical importance".[2]

In 1848, Switzerland, with gratitude due as well to other European rebels, was successful in the establishment of the first representative democracy with some weak direct-democratic elements. Thus, in September 1848, the first Swiss federal constitution was the subject of a vote. This required of all cantons that they insured a minimum of direct democracy. The canton of Zurich, "rigidly" ruled in representational-democratic manner since 1831, did not comply with this proposal until the fall of 1865. The liberal government council and grand council, mainly in order to take the wind out of the sails of a growing opposition movement, passed the right for 10,000 entitled voters, approximately 15% of all entitled voters, to be allowed to propose a change to the canton constitution and hold a referendum on it.

2 Kleine Zürcher History of the Constitution 1218-2000, published by the State Archive of the Zurich Canton, Zurich, 2000, p. 60.

This instrument, originally regarded as weak and of little relevance, proved to be extremely powerful and efficient only two years later. In November and December of 1867, over 20,000 people of Zurich gathered in huge public meetings and demanded comprehensive state and societal reforms. Within only a few days, in December 1867, 27,000 signatures were amassed for a total revision of the canton constitution. These were presented just before Christmas to the governing federal council who set the date for the demanded referendum already on January 26, 1868. The result was overwhelming. With 50,000 to 7,000 with a election participation of over 90% – ten years before, only a few more than 10% of eligible voters had participated in elections – the people of Zurich voted for a total revision of the constitution which led to the establishment of direct democracy already in a little more than only one year in the canton of Zurich as well as to direct democratic majorities in Zurich's Parliament and government.

In retrospect, the summary is easy for a historian. Thus Meinrad Suter writes about the Zurich power landslide of the 1860s: "The unexpected surge of growth and modernization which set in after the founding of federation in 1848 had to bring about quite necessary political changes with it." The social question as well as the integration of "diametrically opposing powers" was too much for the "rigid representationally-constituted state system". And he concludes: "The amazing politicization of a previously lethargic public in the 1860 decade shows that the time was ripe for a modification of the system"[3].

Many people would see this in a similar way at the European level today. The problems are enormous – from the financial and economic crisis to the inability to control climate warming, from unemployment, the crisis in search for meaning, from the social rift of enormous enrichment of a few and the social fears and impoverishment of many, to the financial problems of the social insurance agencies – , the political modification of the system is long overdue – the citizens generally lethargic in regards to the EU and at risk of succumbing to nationalistic temptations because that is where the only democratic lever to use has been until now.

This could all change now with the ECI. If this instrument is acknowledged by many Europeans as a chance to turn themselves towards the EU, not relinquishing it any longer to economic lobbyists and EU functionaries but to help ones own and the overall interests to break through, then this ECI can become a new beginning for the EU and European democracy.

This is because many people let themselves be mobilized by an officially-recognized instrument which is integrated in the decision-making processes than if there is no chance of official recognition. Let us therefore not underestimate the ECI. Let us fight first for a citizen-friendly implemen-

3 Ibid. p. 57

tation of this pioneer work and let us make use of it for the long-needed democratic EU reconstruction (onset of a truly federalist federal state, two-chamber parliament in Brussels, true European public initiative right) for the humanizing of European commerce and politics. Who knows, perhaps it will be said in a commentary on voting in the year 2025 in regards to Europe like in 1869 in regards to Zurich: “This is the first consistent attempt to implement the idea of a purely popular government into a form correspondent to modern culture proportions.”

Tamara EHS

A European People – Caught in the Act?[1]

Previous speakers have identified some practical challenges to the ECI like an official language translation service and the like.[2] For my part, I would like to raise awareness for even more future challenges – for challenges that effect the way we imagine or even exercise a European democracy: The participants of this summit agree on one important thing, namely that democracy and civil liberties are inseparably linked. In thinking about a transnational – or even "supranational" democracy – and a more direct democracy, we must not forget those civil liberties. Reflecting on a European democracy should go hand in hand with talking about the demos, the people that make this democracy. Who is this European people that should take the initiative in an ECI? Who is this civil society that should be activated?

Gatherings like this summit can also seize the opportunity to identify the shortcomings of the concept of the ECI. A major shortcoming lies in the definition of who is "the European people", of who is allowed to take the initiative. By limiting the initiative to EU citizens – that is to citizens of a Member State – the European Union misses the chance to identify a real transnational people, a European people made up by all permanent EU-residents, a people defined independently from and differently than that of the Member States. The idea of a transnational people still appears rash to many of us – at least as long as this transnational people does not declare itself a nation (and thereby return to the old concepts).[3] But we have

1 Speech given on May 9, 2009. – For more detailed explanations of the ideas raised see Tamara Ehs and Gerd Valchars (2009): Demos statt Ethnos. Plädoyer für ein EU-Volk jenseits des Homo Europaeus, in: Blätter für deutsche und internationale Politik, 4/2009, pp. 85-91; Tamara Ehs and Jürgen Busch, EUuropa als Rechtsgemeinschaft, in: Tamara Ehs (ed.) Hans Kelsen und die Europäische Union. Erörterungen moderner (Nicht-)Staatlichkeit, Baden-Baden: Nomos 2008, pp. 95-111.

2 Cf. Theo Schiller in this volume.

3 Being stuck to the classical notion Claus Leggewie recently called the Europeans the "größte Noch-Nicht-Volk der Erde" (Claus Leggewie (2009): Schlachtfeld Europa. Transnationale Erinnerung und europäische Identität, in: Blätter für deutsche und internationale Politik, 2/2009, pp. 81-93).

to rid ourselves of the historical, ethnocentric and cultural prejudices (the doctrine of the "Kulturnation").[4] Instead, we should get back to a normative notion of the people, deriving from the general theory of the state as, for instance, elaborated by Hans Kelsen in his critical review on Immanuel Kant's writings.

As worked out in Perpetual Peace (1795) Kant thinks of a "Weltbürgerrecht" (cosmopolitan right), of combining cosmopolitanism and democracy, of people having rights not because they are citizens but just because they are human beings. Therefore, the "inclusion of the other" (Jürgen Habermas)[5] is not based on philanthropy or mercy but constitutes a human right. This is more topical than ever in the globalisation age when people transcend borders and even take residence in a country other than in which they were born in and/ or hold citizenship more often than ever before in history. It is indeed the legacy of Kant's ideas on cosmopolitanism not to treat the guest as a mere guest but as a potential member of our society and polity.[6] Furthermore, this seems to be highly topical also with regard to the challenge already posed to the concept of traditional nation states by the process of European integration.

If our resolution adopted here in Salzburg is meant to also be a working paper to give us a starting point for the discussions of the next year, we should put our ideas of a transnational civil society as a transnational people on the agenda, especially if we have the host institute's motto "Law and the weaker party" in mind!

I think of the ECI as a real trans-European civic activity of a European solidarity in the making: Whosoever living permanently under the rule of the legal system of the EU is subject to its norms and therefore should be allowed to take the initiative. There is no need to cite the common roots of antiquity, Christianity or Enlightenment (and therefore drawing the line to any "other", be it Islam or whatever) to detect the European people. It is the link constituted by their subjection to common EU-norms that unites individuals permanently resident in the EU to a European people.

Why shouldn't we argue for extending the right to table an ECI to all people lawfully residing in the European Union? Excluding permanent residents and thereby accepting the divergence between the political community and the actual resident population, i.e. between the rulers and the ruled, recalls pre-democratic systems of government. In contrast, allowing all permanent residents to participate in the ECI would be a first step towards a European people in a modern conception of the EU. The

4 Cf. Thomas Schmitz (2007): Globalisation, International Law, People and State, in The Federalist 49(3)/2007, pp. 210-222.

5 Jürgen Habermas (1996): Die Einbeziehung des Anderen. Studien zur politischen Theorie, Frankfurt am Main: Suhrkamp.

6 For further details cf. Seyla Benhabib (2004): The Rights of Others. Aliens, Residents, and Citizens, Cambridge: UP.

legal criterion for participation would be the right of residence in a Member State, which consequently means including third-country nationals. These people (approximately 18.5 million) contribute to the economic and social life of the European Union and they are subject to EU norms. But concerning political rights they are still excluded from taking part in the European Union. Why not at least allowing them to take the initiative?

Hard to believe, but this idea is not that far-fetched:[7] The European Union Parliament and the Commission have generally promoted an extension of voting rights to third-country nationals but have also argued that imposing it on member states would fall outside Community competence. In 1992, the Council of Europe adopted the Convention on the Participation of Foreigners in Public Life at Local Level, which entered into force in 1997. Including a local franchise for all foreign nationals after five years of residence (Art. 6, para. 38) it "remains a landmark when it comes to the international legal protection of the civil and political rights of non-citizens"[8] but has not been ratified by all member states yet and has had no major impact. This is also true for Recommendation 1500 (Participation of Immigrants and Foreign Residents in Political Life) by the Parliamentary Assembly of the Council of Europe passed in 2001 and adopted in 2002.

Nonetheless, a lot has already been accomplished: even a look historically shows us that the practice of enfranchising third-country nationals was quite common in the USA, the prime example of a country of immigration. Many US-states permitted alien residents to vote in state or federal elections. This was only stopped in the 1920s. But today there are political campaigns for introducing a local franchise again for non-citizens; and some states, e.g. Maryland, have already adopted this policy.

Worldwide there are 45 democracies allowing third-country nationals to cast a ballot in communal, regional and in some countries even in the national elections.[9] It would just be appropriate for a post-national(ist) polity and immigration entity like the EU to follow this modern way of responding to modern lifestyle. People are not stuck to one country anymore for their lifetime, they feel and act according to different (cultural, political, religious etc.) affiliations at the same time[10], there is voluntary or forced

7 For the following cf. Rainer Bauböck (2005): Expansive Citizenship: Voting Beyond Territory and Membership, in: Political Science and Politics, 38(4)/2005, pp. 683-687.

8 Patrick Thornberry, María Amor Martín Estébanez (2004): Minority Rights in Europe: A Review of the Work and Standards of the Council of Europe, Council of Europe, p. 546.

9 Cf. André Blais, Louis Massicotte and Antoine Yoshinika (2001): Deciding who has the Right to Vote: A comparative Analysis of Election Laws, in: Electoral Studies 20/2001, pp. 41-62.

10 Cf. Sabine Strasser (2009): Bewegte Zugehörigkeiten. Nationale Spannungen, transnationale Praktiken und transversale Politik, Wien: Verlag Turia + Kant.

migration, the EU even supports mobility (freedom of movement and residence etc). But at the same time, those mobile seem to be punished for their mobility as they lose their right to vote (most notably in national, i.e. the most important elections) when not being able to show the "right" passport. Although the European Union was able to weaken the old division between citizens and non-citizens in some respects by e.g. passing directives like the one on the Status of third-country nationals who are long-term residents (2003/109/EC) the right to political participation remains the privilege of the national. This is one of the most problematic democratic deficits, reducing the quality of democracy by reducing the quantity of people allowed to participate.

The ECI offers a historical chance to close the gap between the ideals and the real democracy. Critics already say that it is just a symbolic plaything, that the people have just been given a playpen because the ECI will only be a very first step in the law-making process which is always launched by the Commission. Yes, unfortunately, it is quite weak but it is also a first step towards a legitimate polity that requires the agreement of the sovereign, the people. But who is "the people"? Why should we go on denying a European people just because it is not the "classical national people" that we have been used to for over 200 years? Denying a transnational European people means depriving it of sovereignty.

What is our vision of a European democracy? For my part, it is a liberal democracy as a polity of inclusion: a democratic polity as a community of individuals who are subject to common laws. Therefore, citizenship and the right to vote should be decoupled to overcome the traditional definition of "the people" by resolving the nexus of "Abstimmungsgemeinschaft" (demos) and "Abstammungsgemeinschaft" (ethnos).[11] Then, the politico-legal notion "people" would be applied to the population lawfully residing in the member states of the European Union. With the Treaty of Lisbon, we already see the hints of recognition of some kind of transnational people by the ECI. The ECI's legal requirement of territorial distribution contributes to the emerging of European civil networks – which is possible in the age of the internet. Therefore we have quite modern instruments but at the same time we have an understanding of "the people" in the style of the 19th century.

My appeal: If we are specifying the shortcomings of the ECI or if we formulate some recommendations for further discussions we should not miss the chance to state that we are aware of a more principal problem when it comes to democracy. Democracy is about achieving an identity of rulers and ruled, of people acted upon and people acting. The ECI could be one first step to close the existing undemocratic gap.

11 Cf. Dieter Oberndörfer (2005): Deutschland in der Abseitsfalle. Politische Kultur in Zeiten der Globalisierung, Freiburg: Herder.

Literature

Bauböck, Rainer (2005): Expansive Citizenship: Voting Beyond Territory and Membership, in Political Science and Politics 38(4)/2005, pp. 683-687.

Benhabib, Seyla (2004): The Rights of Others. Aliens, Residents, and Citizens, Cambridge: UP.

Blais, André / *Massicotte*, Louis / *Yoshinika*, Antoine (2001): Deciding who has the Right to Vote: A comparative Analysis of Election Laws, in Electoral Studies 20/2001, pp. 41-62.

Ehs, Tamara / *Valchars*, Gerd (2009): Demos statt Ethnos. Plädoyer für ein EU-Volk jenseits des Homo Europaeus, in Blätter für deutsche und internationale Politik 4/2009, pp. 85-91.

Ehs, Tamara / *Busch*, Jürgen (2008): EUropa als Rechtsgemeinschaft, in Tamara Ehs (ed.) Hans Kelsen und die Europäische Union. Erörterungen moderner (Nicht-)Staatlichkeit, Baden-Baden: Nomos 2008, pp. 95-111.

Habermas, Jürgen (1996): Die Einbeziehung des Anderen. Studien zur politischen Theorie, Frankfurt am Main: Suhrkamp.

Leggewie, Claus (2009): Schlachtfeld Europa. Transnationale Erinnerung und europäische Identität, in Blätter für deutsche und internationale Politik 2/2009, pp. 81-93.

Oberndörfer, Dieter (2005): Deutschland in der Abseitsfalle. Politische Kultur in Zeiten der Globalisierung, Freiburg: Herder.

Schmitz, Thomas (2007): Globalisation, International Law, People and State, in The Federalist 49(3)/2007, pp. 210-222.

Strasser, Sabine (2009): Bewegte Zugehörigkeiten. Nationale Spannungen, transnationale Praktiken und transversale Politik, Wien: Verlag Turia + Kant.

Thornberry, Patrick / *Estébanez*, María Amor Martín (2004): Minority Rights in Europe: A Review of the Work and Standards of the Council of Europe, Council of Europe.

Johannes W. PICHLER

An Initiative Initiator's Experience

I. Think positive – Prelude

www.we-change-europe.eu is the name of the initiative I represent. It is a battle cry for a better and more democratic Europe. To make you aware of the value of battle cries in general, I'll state immediately that there is no change in sight even now. But as a legal historian by profession, I am full of hope that times are changing. Why? Because history has demonstrated that times have always changed for the better. No one can deny that we have it much better than our ancestors had it. So it makes sense to continue to work for a better Europe. No doubt democracy is always the better way because it is in line with self-determination.

We have met to discuss our problems very openly for the purpose of:

- providing future generations with our ways and means to succeed (or to fail)
- protecting them against the traps which we have suffered from
- allowing them to learn from our mistakes
- giving them the opportunity to draw the right conclusions
- providing the EU authorities with an overall picture of the barriers to democracy.

So...

II. Funny story, isn't it?

... I will deliver a shamelessly open view of my case, initially in the form of a story that could be seen as a bizarre and funny tale. Warning: don't laugh too loudly or too early as your laughter will echo.

As an editor and author of a book on the initiative process, I will, no doubt, become more analytical as we go on later during the conference.

Let me begin my private story on a positive note. My idea is one in support of Europe and of the Europeanization of the Europeans by introducing direct democracy. Let me emphasize that I most assertively stand for a pro-European and pro-active position. And let me additionally emphasize that I have done all my work for free.

Fortunately, I held the Chair as Professor for European Legal Developments and so both my academic vision and my activism go together.

Most fortunately, I have very good friends who were so overwhelmed and convinced by my obsessive pro-European, pro-citizen and pro-direct democracy enthusiasm that they equipped me with significant private grants to bring forth an all-European citizens' initiative platform and to introduce my own initiatives on this platform.

Fortunately, they supported my pro-European activity altruistically, idealistically and without conditions except for one: I was forced to give my best to put Europe back into the hands of the citizens. This I did. While I did not necessarily succeed in the latter, I certainly gave my best, my all.

Fortunately then, I was able to locate the best initiative campaigners. Since there is no precedence in Europe on initiatives, I found them in the USA. The firm I committed to working with was highly successful in launching and achieving their American initiatives. Even those considered unachievable. Let me confess, I was very impressed by the key players of this organization. I liked them from the first moment. So, hurray, I thought, let's change Europe together. Unfortunately, I thought that were brothers-in-arms, since they indicated they had European roots and shared my desire for a human rights-based Europe and to convert Europeans to the idea of self-government by initiative. Nevertheless, things turned out very differently. I am hesitant to name them since I don't like dropping names, even as impressive as they are but, in the end, they were certainly the only winners.

III. Still a funny story?

The end of "fortunately"; from now on, I must add the prefix "un" to "fortunately".

Unfortunately, they promised that the top contenders would transform the challenge into a self runner – for the right amount of money, of course. Furthermore, they promised to take the role as general entrepreneur, which sounded great to me, being more of a philosopher than a CEO. They showed me their numbers and I, as a naive professor among real global players, assumed this was a good deal.

Unfortunately, the experts showed themselves to be bloody beginners at least on the European front. So they solicited assistance from their European branch, or better said, from their European mother. Now I had two world top consultants on board, real top dogs with all the financial consequences and with lots of worries, chiefly, which one of them would actually assume leadership.

Unfortunately, the campaigning firms, as general entrepreneurs, took over the responsibility of hiring fund raisers. The American sector, obviously siding with a good friend, proposed a Swiss top gun with a serious background in the World Economic Forum: "Johannes, he is the one with the best rolodex in Europe! He has the personal cell phone number of Bill Gates!". Okay, the professor from elsewhere was impressed. So they agreed to contract this gentleman and I got a fund raiser, as they said, with an outstanding reputation among the richest decision-makers in Europe. Well, the new hotshot on board, surprisingly enough, refused from the start to be a fund raiser. And he produced exactly one email consisting of about fifty lines and charged our association for two months of work. Talk began of a lawsuit but a lawsuit is not exactly what one needs when rolling out an all-European campaign, both intense and exhausting. We, the European side and I, decided mutually not to sue.

Unfortunately, both campaigner sectors burned through the money using totally inadequate means, much of which were consulting fees without action or real deliverables. Thinking and rethinking their strategy and thinking about me took weeks and weeks, during which the clock on our taxi meter was running on. The association was paying for a corps of consultants, most of whom I never saw, most of them costing between 400 and 600 US Dollars, not per day but per hour, of course. Worse yet, the Americans thought it good enough to keep us informed about the bill, since they spent hours and hours thinking about my project and shared my concerns – without informing me of exactly what the content of their thinking was. And I was certainly not allowed to ask about the results of their thinking. "Whatever maestros do is right, otherwise they wouldn't be maestros".

Unfortunately, in addition to this, we burned through a lot of money on research on whether my suggested issues possessed the power to get the Europeans to make up their political minds and to raise their voices. My suggested issues were

1) Are the Europeans committed to speaking out and voting on an initiative regarding the issue of EU enlargement?
2) Are Europeans attracted to the idea of electing the EU president directly and on their own?

So my consultants hired an excellent research firm. By the way, the Los Angeles-based research firm was personally intimately involved with the campaigner. This is how I ended up in some sort of clan. Sure, I finally realized that but not until after we had signed a contract. By the way, number 2, the focus groups research throughout Europe was done very professionally, so no criticism of that. Actually, for me as an academic, this was the most advantageous part of the whole process. By the way, number 3, however, the research period lasted months with nothing happening on the consultant side while the taxi meter still ran on and on.

Not surprising for anyone familiar with the Euro barometer, both issues proved to be highly attractive and feasible, in particular, issue nr. 1. Nevertheless, the American campaigning firm favored a third, green issue, which indeed figured very well and seemed appropriate to any European. I have to confess, I was impressed by the ranking of this issue itself. But the suggested core campaign slogans: "We, the initiative, initiate that Europeans unplug the charger, now!" and "We, the initiative, initiate that Europeans use energy saving light bulbs from now on!" were ridiculous. You know, you can read those suggestions on any flyer of your local energy provider over the last decade. So the European mother opposed the campaigning strategy of the American daughter. Not very funny for the paying consultee to see his consultants fighting each other, you know, and the taxi meter, still running on. Well, the competence conflict caused another significant delay. And when I, very uneasy after months, requested the clear and full-scale campaign plan, I got a short campaign paper which said nothing and was far beneath even my own knowledge. So I got upset. Soon after, I was informed of another effort, a multi-million dollar commercial campaign planned by my American sector that was driven and financed by the greatest producer of energy saving light bulbs in Europe. I became furious. And I retracted the contract immediately.

Unfortunately, I continued the campaign with the remaining European partner. In their defense, they strictly followed the German standards of formality. Nevertheless, I add an "unfortunately" because they did not show any better results. They were very correct and we had an outstanding and very likable political consultant on board. But a decent warning by the American partner turned out to be right on: "Johannes, the Germans have no idea how to run an initiative campaign". True, they were top of the line, let's say the Deutsche Bank or Mercedes Benz in advertising. Indeed, they were great offline advertisers, but a pan-European campaign can only be carried out online. So the efforts we made were all in vain. We organized media conferences throughout Europe, but there was no response. I got just a handful of voters on our voting portal. But the EU requirement is of at least one million votes, as Art 11.4 TEU prescribes. Furthermore, together we learned that our campaigners' network did not work. For a press conference at the Deutsche Bundespressekonferenz in Berlin, worth several thousand Euros, they supposedly contacted approximately 400 journalists. Three journalists showed up; only one was of the 400. The others simply had heard via the official EU event calendar that there was to be a breakfast. Things did not go any better with press conferences in Brussels or London. Media conferences worth about 12,000 Euros and still we had no resonance. It cannot have been a good experience for them either, but it was the Initiative's money that was wasted.

Because academics are trained to investigate failure, I wondered whether my issues were the right issues for us or not. Even when the above-mentioned research proved that the issues are of the utmost importance to the European community, I doubted myself. The answer is obviously found in the middle: Europeans are definitely not easily alarmed but the decision to campaign offline was wrong. So we let our relationship fizzle without making any fuss.

Unfortunately the donation money was running out gradually so I took on the burden of campaigning on my own with help from my small team. And this was the beginning of a long and exhausting road, but we still continue. And we will continue further, we promise. Our Europe is worth it.

One lesson learned: a European initiative campaign spanning 23 languages and diverse cultures can only be done online. And this is how we campaign now. In the meantime, we had worked with another expensive consultant, one that advertised himself as an outstanding Web 2.0 expert and solemnly promised to cause a "virile", rocket-like explosion of voters signing up. Result? A catastrophe! They foresaw attracting at least 100,000 signatories. And? A mere two hundred signatures were gathered in from obscure sources. At the end of their disgrace, we were still a mere 99,732 votes away from their declared goal and 999,732 votes away from the 1,000,000 requirement under Art 11.4 TEU/ToLisbon. Now it really was time for a lawsuit, finally. Thus recommend that this Initiative Agency, about which we must later discuss, should also take the responsibility for compiling a blacklist. We must protect further initiatives against simply getting ripped-off by liars and cheats.

IV. Stupid, it's the money! Guess who found that out? Me!

So let me end up the story part with a last word about finances (you got it right, so very much is about money!). We have contacted hundreds of very wealthy individuals and dozens of very well-funded foundations to support us to affiliate the European citizens with their Union. But only one of them contributed with an amount of several thousand Euros. This lady's company ran into serious economic trouble shortly thereafter. It doesn't help her that much, but, being grateful, I do buy her products ever since, namely car tires. None of the others billionaires invested a single lousy Euro to support this same EU which has helped them to greatly increase their profits over decades.

Got the message? Initiative idealists have to face the fact that they are committed to take the long, long way to Tipperary.

You, Commission, face it, too, that a public EU funding and supporting scheme must be provided; otherwise, this instrument works counterproductively. Frustrations of otherwise pro-active Pro-Europeans are the inevitable result.

End of story time.

Theo SCHILLER

Implementing the European Citizens' Initiative – the context of civic participation

The Lisbon treaty will, after final ratification, offer to the European citizens, for the first time, the right to political participation in the form of direct democracy by the European Citizens' Initiative (Art. 11.4). Since a European Citizens' Initiative must be supported by signatures of one million citizens from several member states this will be an important transnational participatory institution and can be of great service to the European Union to develop more sense of a political community than has been achieved in the last decades. An implementation law has to spell out the conditions for making practical use of this direct democratic right. Since this is to be a right of the citizens, it should be logical that citizens can already participate in defining these legal requirements for using this procedure. Therefore, this Salzburg Citizens' Summit of May 2009 gives the great opportunity to help define the needs of citizens which are to be realised in the future ECI Implementation Act.

Some earlier activities of various institutions have already started the process of deliberations on this task. One important contribution has just been provided by the European Parliament which, shortly before the end of its term, accepted a report of its Committee on Constitutional Affairs on principles and details of an implementation law.[1] The EP advocates several very agreeable positions, but some recommendations are still debatable, like the requirement of a rather high number of Member States (one quarter) from which signatures of citizens have to come. One major deficit surely is the silence of the EP on the issues of supporting infrastructure for citizens and civil society groups (mounting an initiative), as has been noted by several contributors to this conference. Such official support will surely be a necessary condition for citizens to successfully employ this new procedure. Yet, support also has to be placed in a broader picture of participatory politics.

---

1 European Parliament resolution of May 7, 2009, requesting the Commission to submit a proposal for a regulation of the European Parliament and of the Council on the implementation of the citizens' initiative (2008/2196(INI)).

The European Citizens' Initiative can unfold as an important right and instrument for civic participation in the European Union. As is well known, however, from the theory of participatory democracy, many challenges have to be met to bring this right to practical life. Official infrastructure support can and must provide basic assistance, which has yet to be linked to other major challenges for initiative activities. At least three more important dimensions of a direct democratic procedure like ECI are relevant here:

Civic competence will be the basis of all participation, including information, motivation and the capacity to act politically in cooperation with others for common goals.

Transnational/European civic activity will be the specific feature of participation in the context of the European Union which requires specific competences and cooperating mechanisms.

Experience in direct democracy procedures, particularly with the agenda initiative participation model which the European Citizens' Initiative follows, will help citizens to make use of this form of procedure.

Putting the ECI into practice will work much better if these dimensions of European political action are well developed, and therefore, elements of official support for citizens' initiatives should be linked as closely as possible to stimulate these conditions of European participation. When we look at these dimensions in more detail, several aspects stand out: first, some *general elements* of infrastructure will be required; procedures and legislative proposals always imply some *legal issues*; European actors have to interact in a great number of *languages*; co-operation in modern Europe will only be possible with the help of *e-communication*; participation connecting millions of people also needs support of the *media*; substantial amounts of *financial resources* will be required.

Major elements of official support:

The most general feature of support should be an independent European Initiative Agency funded by the European Commission and the European Parliament with the task of administering in a neutral and fair way the procedural requirements of an initiative and giving advice to initiators. One part of this agency should be an independent section providing legal advice. In order to handle the language dimension it will also be necessary to have the translation services of the European institutions available for the initiative process. Support for an e-communication infrastructure will be crucial to enable initiating groups to communicate policy proposals Europe-wide; also the collection of signatures should be made possible by e-technology. To leave the provision of an e-infrastructure completely to the groups of initiators would reproduce great social inequalities of different interests and would result in undue advantages for powerful and well-endowed organisations. For the same reasons, at least some financial support for initiatives should be provided, maybe in the form of flat payments or in step-by-step-increases.

As has been mentioned above, these support features can only work if they converge with and stimulate civil society participation engaging in European Citizens' Initiative activities.

Aspects of civic competence:

A general dimension of civic competence for European policy proposals will be civic education in a two-fold way: a) political knowledge must be distributed on European politics generally, i.e. on problems relevant at the EU level, EU jurisdiction, and political decision-making in the EU; b) knowledge of the ECI as an agenda initiative procedure and the specific rules and conditions for using it. To make progress in disseminating such information, civic education agencies in the European Member States and the media should become active in a multiplying function. Certainly political learning by practicing the ECI right and procedure will also help in this process. As to legal issues of an EC Initiative, the provision of legal advice by an EU agency should be supplemented by networks of independent legal advisors in the Member States which can assist an initiative. A major problem which cannot be solved by EU language services will result from the need for multi-language communication in advocating initiative goals since one language only (English) will not be enough. Extending language competence in European societies can only work as a long-term process. It may be that the necessary dissemination of competence in e-communication will proceed faster, particularly with young people. An additional need for initiators will be media competence in using media information and, even more, for stimulating media activity which can help to bring about public debates on the European policy issues involved. Surely it is self-evident that for all these activities financial and manpower resources will be needed which cannot be provided completely by official EU support. Thus, knowledge and experience in fundraising will also be an important dimension of civic competence.

Aspects of transnational/European civic activity:

The great value which an ECI can contribute to European politics is transnational European political activity. This implies the important and general challenge for the first initiators of finding partners in other EU Member States and establishing European networks, at least in a minimum number of states. Within such networking activities, the relevance of issues for different Member States has to be deliberated as well as discussing common goals. Legal aspects of an initiative may often include the exchange of legal information and learning of supranational, European legal state of affairs. The language dimension becomes very concrete in the need for multi-language and cross-language communication within European initiative networks on the specific issues at stake which also involves learning about specific problem patterns and political cultures of various member states.

For transnational networking, e-communication will stand out as a very special and valuable function. The most innovative element of infrastructure should be an independent, electronic *Initiative Exchange Platform* which will offer Europe-wide and general opportunities to list new initiative posters, and in this way to inform potential network partners and invite their cooperation. For setting up a backbone infrastructure like this, official EU support will be particularly important.

In the field of media communication, there will also be need of transnational interactions. First, more information should be disseminated through journalists to make the ECI procedure better known and more popular; second, discussions on specific issues and initiatives will have to be carried in the media with a transnational perspective which will gradually contribute to a richer public community on European affairs.

Activities of this kind can only be realised with some resources for which cross-border fundraising will be adequate and more difficult at the same time. Since transnational fundraising also needs more trust, it will be helped by advocating and achieving transparency of campaign finances.

Aspects of direct democracy experience:

For the ECI as a right and a procedure of direct democracy to be practiced, general conditions will improve if direct democracy can also be used on the national or at least regional and local level in the Member States. Just as citizens have experienced national elections, they will feel better acquainted with a new European instrument if they know it from home. This may apply for referendums and initiatives at large as well as for the specific model of agenda initiatives like the ECI. Yet in many European Member States, not much direct democracy could be experienced.[2] Therefore, it seems reasonable to advocate, at minimum, the introduction of agenda initiative procedures in all Member States, and possibly more than this, like full-scale citizens' initiatives and citizen-demanded referendums. This, again, will serve to stimulate media information on agenda initiatives and other forms of direct democracy. With regard to financial resources, this will be an opportunity for also recommending some public financial support for national agenda initiatives as an institutional complement to the ECI. This will, for sure, be an ambitious goal to open up debates about introducing direct democracy rights also on the national level of Member

2 For more information on this approach: Schiller, Theo (2009): Approaches to Developing Direct Democracy in the European Union, in: Pichler, Johannes W. (Ed.): Direct Democracy in the European Union, 107 – 117

States. But some institutional correspondence between the European Union and national political communities will help to develop political participation and democracy at large. There should be an elaborated institutional environment for attracting citizens' participation at all levels. Official support for ECI infrastructure will work better if linked to democratic institutions which provide opportunities of political engagement rather than blocking or undermining civic activities.

In summary, the European Citizens' Initiative can only be brought to life with the support of a good implementation law. It has great potential as an instrument of citizen involvement in European politics but for a procedure to be practiced in a continent with 450 million people and 27 Member States with many languages, major obstacles have to be overcome. The overall goal must be to attract real citizens' participation on European policy issues. Official support measures of EU institutions for using this initiative procedure should best be targeted to the many barriers which refrain Europeans from becoming active European citizens. And to make support measures work, the other major dimensions of a democratic culture of participation also have to be developed. Thus, infrastructure assistance will best serve if civic competence, transnational civic activity and broader experience in direct democracy can be strengthened in a consonant way.

We all know that the European Citizens' Initiative has been much criticised as an agenda initiative which has the limits of only "inviting the EU Commission" to present draft legislation, i.e. to bring an issue on the European agenda, and not providing a track to a referendum vote. This is surely true, but we only have the ECI as a provision in the Treaty of Lisbon, and there will not be more for some time to come. One should, however, consider a developmental approach: when the ECI is put into practice, initiators and signatories will in fact experience these limits and quite likely they will take up this criticism again in the practical political arena. A first step like the ECI very often also provides the opportunity to ask for more. We have to leave it to the European citizens and particularly to civil society to make political demands for more far-reaching institutions of direct democracy in Europe.

Appendix

Salzburg Manifesto for the European Citizens' Initiative (ECI) under Art 11.4 TEUnV-ToLisbon adressed to the European Union

Today, May 9, 2009, on Europe Day, European citizens met in Salzburg, Austria, to assess the preparations towards the implementation of the European Citizens' Initiative Right as proposed by the Lisbon Treaty (TEU, Art 11.4). Co-hosted by the Initiative & Referendum Institute Europe (Marburg) and the Austrian Institute for European Law and Policy (Salzburg), the Citizens' Initiative Summit welcomed the decision by the European Parliament on the pending implementation of Art 11.4, the first transnational direct democratic procedure in history. This will put the citizens on an equal standing with the EU Council and the EU Parliament regarding the right to start legislative action on the EU level.

It is the understanding of the European Citizens' Initiative Summit that this new, innovative citizen right is an inclusive, integrative and transnational procedure. As an agenda initiative, it is neither a petition (which already exists in respect to the EU parliament) nor a full citizen initiative leading to a popular vote. It establishes for the very first time a direct legislative channel for European citizens.

The Salzburg Summit applauds the clear decision by the European Parliament on May 7, 2009 to agree on a Resolution for a citizen-friendly implementation process. This demonstrates the will of Parliament to put citizens on an equal footing with the Parliament and the Council, thereby establishing a modern representative democracy on the transnational level including direct democratic rights. The Summit however understands that several aspects outlined in the EP resolution need further improvement including the number of signatory countries, which at present seems too high. Furthermore, the Summit suggests that the time frames proposed in the EP resolution are too short and should be extended.

In light of the work on the regulative aspects of the implementation law which now requires additional fine-tuning and the basis of a citizen-friendly understanding of the new Right, the Summit clearly states that the new European Citizens' Initiative Right will have to be complemented with a comprehensive supportive infrastructure, including the establishment of a European Citizen Initiative Office as well as financial and administrative advice and support across Europe.

The Salzburg Citizens' Initiative Summit agreed in particular on the following:

If the European Citizens' Initiatives (ECI) are to become a useful right, they need a citizen-friendly design including regulatory actions and efficient proactive support from the EU.

Due to the fact that the European Citizens' Initiative Right is constructed as a mechanism for the input of political proposals from the citizens of Europe, the EU Commission should in principle affirm the initiatives as a support procedure for better and more formal identification of the concrete concerns of those citizens.

The EU is therefore invited to create a proactive guiding, supporting, consulting and accompanying entity – known as the ECI Office.

Since the envisioned pan-European initiative activities will inevitably include digital means of communication and signature gathering, the ECI Office is to create appropriate E-systems or adopt and adapt existing E-systems and have these operating under the supervision and scrutiny of the EU.

The implementation regulations have to predict and plan pragmatic models for viable and effective solutions. Since the European Citizens' Initiative Right is an agenda-setting initiative procedure (in contrast to a full citizens' initiative procedure leading to a binding popular vote on substantial issues), complex and costly high official structures using the 27 national authorities should be avoided.

Since the European Citizens' Initiative Right clearly and wisely seeks to facilitate transnational European concerns, any supporting infrastructure should also be located at the transnational European level. National authorities should not need to be used by the EU authorities other than to verify signatures by random control.

Restrictive measures – such as excluding the admissibility of so-called constitutional initiatives or attaching unnecessarily burdensome requirements – must be rejected. The widest range of submissions addressed to the EU Commission is to be welcomed.

Because the underlying concept of Art 11.4 signifies that the ECI is primarily directed at unrepresented or under-represented citizens, free initiatives which apply must necessarily receive basic financial support.

Initiatives funded by public money are obliged to disclose all formal cooperations with other individuals or organizations in respect to financial support.

European Citizens' Initiative Office

Objectives

Europe and its citizens are entering new democratic territory. By the end of 2010 half a billion of Europeans will be get the right to propose new EU legislation – by the means of the new European Citizens' Initiative (Treaty of Lisbon, Article 11.4). For the first time in world history, a transnational, direct-democratic procedure will thus be established and can contribute to an effective democratization of the European Union, which have been often and rightly criticized for its democracy deficit. In order to become an effective tool for all Europeans – not just the powerful and well-organized ones – the new EU Citizens' Initiative Right must bot only become a citizens-friendly provision, but also a encouraging practice supported by a comprehensive infrastructure. This starts with information about the options and limitations of the new citizens' right, continues with training efforts of competent agencies and agents and extends into facilitating of each stage in a European Citizens' Initiative process.

Mission Statement

In order to make all this feasible, a new structure will be established, the European Citizens' Initiative Office [ECIO]. The grand opening of this transnational support office with Headquarters in Salzburg/Austria will take place on Europe Day 2010, May 7-9. The ECIO intends to pro-actively making a difference for a citizen-centered Europe, by supporting all players in the new world of transnational, modern direct democracy,

- **as an independent think tank**
- as a **competence center** based on fine scientific and journalistic experience among the persons in leadership
- as **a documentation center**
- as a **venue for "stakeholders"** of the new process in civil society, science, media, politics, administration and commerce
- as a **non-partisan platform for activities** regarding the new, transnational, direct-democratic practices
- as an **information hub for citizens** from all over Europe who are considering starting an initiative

- as a **support center for initiative groups** which are waiting in the wings, or, as the case may be, in an implementation phase

The European Citizens' Initiative Office [ECIO] is just the beginning of a comprehensive trans-EU democracy infrastructure which will offer intermediate-term assistance in many smaller and larger ways and will also include official support mechanisms from the EU itself. Because it will take some time, however, to formulate the purpose and terms of reference for such an official infrastructure and to line up the respective measures, the European Citizens' Initiative Office is determined to make a start and views itself as inspiration and impetus for the modern support of democracy in Europe of the 21st century.

Modes of Operation

1. The "European Citizens' Initiative Office" operates as an association under Austrian law with Headquarters in Salzburg, called the ECIO, which intends to assume the responsibilities as described above.
2. The ECIO will be operated in a non-partisan and non-profit manner and directed by persons with key competences on this topic.
3. The Office and its co-workers are assisted by an advisory board which summons qualified experts and high-ranking individuals on the topic and with representatives from institutions who deal with the transacting of European initiatives, with representatives of support organizations and representatives of the EU Commission.
4. The ECIO assumes the responsibilities described above and considers itself a transnational center for the new EU citizens' right of the European Citizens' Initiative according to TEUnv-ToLisbon.

office@initiative-office.eu
Mönchsberg 2a
5020 Salzburg

Executive Board:
Univ.Prof. Dr. Johannes W. Pichler (Chair Uni Graz: European Legal Developments)
Bruno Kaufmann (President IRI Europe)
Dr. Anne-Marie Sigmund (MEESC)
Andreas Gross (MP)

Andreas GROSS / Bruno KAUFMANN / Johannes W. PICHLER / Anne-Marie SIGMUND

The European Citizens' Inititiative Consultation Process (Art 11.4 TEU)

Impulses and suggestions of the European Citizens' Initiative Office (ECIO)

I. Introduction: our pro-active premises regarding the new "initiative legislation"

With Art 11.4, the European Union for the first time is formally given a legislative means of right of proposal for citizens.

The European Citizens' Initiative (ECI) offers a unique win-win opportunity for European democracy, the strengthening of European citizenship, the legitimizing and anchoring of the EU as well as the unique chance for the EU Commission of a new beginning in the difficult relationship until now with EU citizens.

We consider the European Citizens' Initiative a first step towards a representational transnational democracy in Europe. By way of creating an initial element of direct democracy [PAI], people power can be positioned at a transnational level and the existent representative democracy can be made more representative.

Further reflection on the integration of more powerful instruments of direct democracy, like a European constitutional referendum could be the fruit of positive experiences with the Citizens' Initiative. Both of these would be extraordinarily helpful for democracy as well as for Europe.

The European Citizens' Initiative is potentially a suitable instrument for use in countering the frequently heard complaint that European democracy is not sufficiently legitimized and much too estranged from the Union citizens. Whether this potential can be perceived and put to use will be dependent on whether the implementation legislation is designed so that the instrument is indeed used by Union citizens and thus perceived as their instrument. Only EU democracy which is used and experienced enables the effective identification of citizenry with the EU and can only in this way contribute to EU integration.

Only a truly useful and utilized and thus a vital law for the European Citizens' Initiative will develop a European force which builds the identity of citizens.

This kind of European Citizens' Initiative, however, implies that no over-regulation and no unnecessary hurdles will be created and simultaneously, that initiative-promoting structures will be further developed which can prevent the freedom to use this citizen right from becoming a privilege of only a few organizations that possess the necessary resources.

Of course, the allowance for the European legal principle of commensurability in view of implementation of the European initiative, which as we know is only an indirect, merely agenda-setting initiative legislation, signifies that the necessary effort for this must be kept within limits.

At the same time, the European Citizens' Initiative (ECI) offers the unique chance until now for Europe to write world constitutional history and take up a leading position with the first, transnational, direct-democratic right. However, in order for this pioneer accomplishment to truly be able to be used and claimed by all committed Europeans, it should not be dependent on pre-requisites which are unachievable for normal Europeans.

Should the success of the ECI be possible in the end, thanks to a careful, supportive implementation of it, then immeasurable advantages for European integration will have been created. We wish at this point to stress the following advantages which the EU needs more than ever today:

- a strengthened European integration process,
- a more discourse-friendly European public sphere
- a more experiential European identity-development
- a massive increase of transnational legitimacy

II. Regarding an effective European Citizens' Initiative Legislation and the related tendencies suggested in the Commission's Green Paper

Positive Tendencies

In late 2009 the European Commission launched a Green Paper on the ECI regulation and conducted a brief public consultation. Hundreds of organizations, authorities and individual citizens participated in this important process, which was followed-up by a hearing in Brussels on February 22, 2010. The new European Citizens' Initiative Office with Headquarters in Salzburg/Austria participated in pro-actively in this process and provided it's recommendations to the Commission both during the consultation periode and at the Brussels hearing. This article summarized the background for the recommendations as well as the proposals of the European Citizens' Initiative Office as such.

We considered the consultation paper (GP) of the Commission presented in late 2009 to be a highly promising basis for discussion. Even though the Commission in the GP shows itself to be flexible in form and discursive and represents several possible directive approaches, still the GP is unmistakably moving in a carefully considered direction which we appreciate and support. The Commission has generally recognized what there is to do in order to develop a pan-European instrument, transcending as well as integrating the Member States, which links the European citizens directly with the EU and is able to induce pan-European thought and pan-European learning processes – which is what Europe has perhaps the most need of today.

It could, of course, be that governments which view this development with skepticism might try to enter in as "middlemen" between citizens and the Commission by way of involvement in the process. This would be successful for States to the degree that it should not be successful to create a pan-European process for the collection of signatures, in which the roll of the Member States is limited to the certification of the signatures.

Clearly positive in our evaluation is the position suggested by the GP related to the legitimacy of initiatives: this should be cautiously formulated so that no unnecessary hurdles are created and the inherent dignity of the initiative concern can flow into the Commission's treatment after successful submission of signatures.

Such an approach makes sense. A comprehensive examination of legitimacy extending further than an examination of competence would have to be linked with a direct right of access to a decision of the European Court of Justice (ECJ) because of the appeal requirement – with uncertain outcome and the danger that the fronts have already hardened before an initiative was able to be truly launched. Legitimacy hurdles which are too early and too high would call the entire process into question as well as the integrity of the EU Commission, or, as the case may be, the Citizens' Initiative, itself.

Thus it is to be recommended that the formal access to the European Citizens' Initiative right be left as wide open as possible and to signal to the initiative committee at best that an implementation of a concern might however be called into question on grounds of violation of human rights.

It should be possible within the framework of freedom of religion and conscience, the freedom of expression and the freedom of assembly for an initiative to present its concern to a European public and convince it thereof. Thus the EU would be given the singular chance even in a marginal case to demonstrate to this very same public the pan-European canon of legal values and principles upon which it rests itself. The Commission cannot ask for a better possibility than to present itself in marginal cases with regards to content to a pan-European public which has become very observant. It can only be in the interest of the EU Commission for it to present itself openly and with conviction in its organizational political responsibility.

Critical Tendencies

There are parts, however, in the consultation paper which could turn the young instrument from the offset into an ineffectual and above all, untrustworthy medium. Should the Commission have already determined by way of the GP that there should be no pro-active support, financing and mentoring of European Citizens' Initiatives, then their own ambitions in favor of a more democratic European democracy would immediately be called into question – and the commitment to a citizen-friendly implementation of the ECI article degenerate into a lip service.

The danger looms then that the same situation will arise which has already taken place like with the seemingly admirable phrase of equality BEFORE the law in other areas, like in equality of gender. Only through a civil empowerment by way of a factual establishment of equality THROUGH legislation will it be possible to hinder the forward projection of inequality, in this case, the political speechlessness and helplessness of many EU citizens. Only the one who disposes over all resources can hinder that this legislation becomes a privilege of organizations which already have the necessary resources at their disposal. That is what we mean when we say: neither may democracy be allowed to become the privilege of a few if it does not want to lose its character.

That is why it is so important to help bring about authenticity in the new legislation by affirmative actions – in other words, through pro-active support measures. This can take place by way of financial backing and/or the creation of practical support mechanisms.

III. Fundamental considerations and suggestions regarding execution legislation for Art 11.4 TEU

For creating an open, pro-active climate of cooperation

The EU Commission now has the singular chance at its disposal to enter for the first time into a direct relationship with the citizens of Europe. The European citizenry is able for the first time to enter in directly at the "Brussels door" by way of the new initiative right. This decision of the "Lisbon Treaty" can be seen and affirmed as a quiet revolution.

One should therefore avoid any systematic regression to a collaboration with the States in this new direct channel. Alert and active citizens are the salt of Europe. Actors who utilize a parliamentary means always demonstrate a formative power in a vital democracy – and should thus be given a warm welcome – supported, yes, even enlivened and encouraged.

They are able to endow the EU with a new inner political strength on a whole which is greater than the direct legitimacy given to the EU.

Discovery of that which is political in the EU through a more conscious political awareness of the citizenry.

Virtues like a sense of citizenry, vigilance and an active participation are being claimed in a louder and strong way on the level of Member States as well as on the sub national level. And there is much about the "Europe of the Citizen" being talked about also at the transnational European level. However, a true change of attitude regarding the possibilities of decision-making participation "from below" was not obvious for a long time. This led among other things to the strengthening of forces which demanded a re-nationalization of European politics. This is because, as long as democracy is almost solely an option for the States, nationalists always have a trump card at their disposal.

The new Citizens' Initiative brings with it however the possibility of an authentic and effective Europe political awareness and transnational democratization. That means, democracy no longer remains restricted to the State but can also develop along the supranational level. Instead of describing the future use of the Citizens' Initiative right first of all as the collating of particular interests, the "political awareness" of the EU as well as the search for a "European common interest" which it makes possible should be at the center of this reform – something which has become urgent in light of the development toward transnational political community (policies) and the required democratic form (polity).

With a hopefully large number of initiatives, a deliberate process can begin at European level in which Europeans are drawn into a politically RIGHT participatory and creative way of acting and draw their own experiences and conclusions from it. When it is possible for us citizens to experience our creative powers in a RIGHT way then we will also award the EU with the legitimacy which the Union is still lacking. Many people will also begin to identify themselves with the EU in this way.

Awaken awareness that now, for the first time, a formal constitutional tool for citizen empowerment exists.

The current, modest agreement known as the "Lisbon Treaty" should not in any way be called a "constitution" after the first (failed) constitutional round; this is why the originally planned legal protection of symbols like flag and hymn is waived in the treaty. However, the treaty has an inherent potential to make citizens aware of their "constitution" if it is possible to bring awareness to us citizens that we, for the first time, have obtained a little piece of constitutional power, institutional power. That means: with the positioning of the initiative at European level, we obtain new motivation for political action because, from this moment on, in this respect, we are on equal footing with the European Parliament and the European Council.

The legitimate, long-standing complaint was that there was no existing European public. Now, however, in the words of Habermas, finally this means has been constituted by which the constituted subject can create itself. "Europe of the Citizens" until now was more of an appeal than description of a reality. Now, with a vital, true democracy, this gulf between expectation and reality can be closed, step-by-step. It is now decisive how wide open the doors are to this constitutional means, in quantity and quality, in order for as many EU citizens as possible to be able to use it in reality, constructively and successfully.

Do not allow the implementation right ever to be devalued by fraudulent fantasies.

The cardinal error of so many legislators is that they are not directed by the positive goals, the formative goals, in regulating the issue but that they waste the energy in contemplating how potential misuse could be hindered. This may not be permitted to happen in the case of the new EU initiative right!

Upon repeated reference to the democratic-political dimension of Art 11.4 TEU, that is why the principle of proportion should be particularly considered. In view of the ECI's modest weight, legally considered, potential minor cases of misuse may not be used as reference to justify reducing the overall potential.

However, it should be awareness and control that that no grave mass attacks and the implicit numbers fraud is allowed to happen. This type of risk cannot be totally ruled out with online processes. But in result, this kind of risk is easily apparent with the technology made available today and in the future; in addition, the interest of criminal circles seems to be small for the manipulation of a process which has no overall financial profit schemes. Having said this, the limited practical experience with e-collecting of signatures will create the need of proper and innovative procedures, developed on step-by-step basis. This is especially important, as a careless rush into going online even with the e-collecting part would offer an easy way for skeptical voices to dicreditate the whole process as such.

Regarding the verification of signatures, it should suffice that the Commission provides those States from which the signatures come with a particular key for sample control-like examination. In order to reduce the potential error quota here, the number of submitted signatures should be reduced.

Keeping an eye on the dimension of the instrument

We recommend to the EU Commission that they not lose sight of essentials in the preparation on regulating the European Citizens' Initiative: the new public right according to Art 11.4 TEU is an agenda initiative and cannot trigger a popular vote on a substantive issue. The instrument is closer to a petition, in legal terms, than to a popular initiative like the ones in many German states or at the national level in Switzerland. Thus a sense of proportion should be kept regarding the requirements and everything aimed at winning over the citizens in the first place for this new possibility of becoming EU-initiating and in this way enabling them to transcend their distance to Brussels.

Simple structures suffice

The process of collecting signatures – crucial for the qualitative as well as the quantitative success – should be carried out in as much of an uncomplicated and integrative way as possible. That means: unnecessary hurdles – like official registration or the notarization of signatures – must be prevented. Simultaneously, the possibilities for signing must be extensive. Along with a carefully conducted and introduced e-collecting process, there should thus also be the option to give one's signature to paper on the street or send it in by letter.

As the European Citizens' Initiative Office is designed to unite scientific competence with practical experience as well as political commitment, extensive comprehension of Europe as well as enthusiasm – we wish to contribute our knowledge and our deep pro-European conviction in order to make the new constitutional means as attractive as possible. Our experience in founding and operating European initiatives could help the Commission to not have to walk down the crooked paths and detours again which we already have left behind us. So it is critical not to overlook that if the new instrument of direct democracy has once been disappointing, it will be difficult then to reanimate it. This democratic start-up must become a success; otherwise Brussels will be barraged by guffaws of laughter from the tabloids with their malicious tendencies regarding the EU.

How many votes at what age and with which country spread? Peripheral question. Create a sliding scale system!

The provision of legitimacy about the instrument of the European Citizens' Initiative will be dependent on how wide the pan-European spread and by how many Citizens' Initiatives are supported. An aspect of the principles of observance of direct democratic manifestations worldwide is that certain minimum participatory quotas must be met.

Hardly one of the systems known to us however would put up with such an incredibly limited "quorum" like Art 11.4 TEU has. Of course, those popular rights strapped with higher hurdles for the triggering of popular votes are of another binding character and caliber of power. The Art 11.4 TEU instrument is – contrary to local opinion until now – not able to force any binding legislative action in the initiators' interest from the Commission.

That is why it is the task here as well to think innovatively about how the integration-fostering and deliberative aspects of future initiative processes could be most cleverly promoted. Thus we recommend to the Commission to look for an open system, a sliding scale system in which initiatives may be accepted even when they do not fulfill the spread criteria in one point but more than fulfill the criteria catalogue in other points.

One example as an illustration: say an initiative in Malta and in Cyprus and in Luxembourg actually fails to fulfill the distribution key of eg 0,2% per counted member state but instead however brings, say, 1.5 million votes together and this from ten or more States and this in addition perhaps even achieving a representative spread of States between Poland and Portugal, then an initiative of this sort should be able to qualify as well. Consequently, a "double" tallying could be considered which weighs the initiatives similarly along the lines of the EU politically real system of qualified majority in regards to the weight of their representativeness.

In sum, we recommend to the Commission not to lock any doors and to open up a maximum of flexibility – also as evidence of the flexibility of the Commission itself.

The discourse process of EU citizens and the EU Commission

Some think the goals of the instrument of Art 11.4 TEU have been reached when an initiative succeeds in becoming part of the Commission's agenda.

We see reaching the goal completely differently. Not whether the Commission has set the one or the other initiative on its agenda and then nicely communicates that they have extensively mulled over the concern of this or that initiative, is the essential point. We consider it more important that the Commission discloses what deliberate effort the Commission is willing to actually undertake, above and beyond the legal question of whether it has (or doesn't have) to bring an initiative of how much quality and quantity onto the agenda. And whether it is prepared to explain to initiatives in a partially and fully open manner what there is about the initiative concerns and why the Commission finds it worth following through on, or which deliberations and upon what grounds the Commission must regret not (or not yet) following through on an initiative.

It will depend on the political acumen of the EU Commission and not on the legal construction as to how it handles initiatives materially. It will depend on the political acumen of European initiatives as to how it handles the EU Commission in order to present their concerns besides the mere completion of formal criteria in a constructive discourse with Brussels and beyond Brussels.

The relationship of Art 11.4 to the petition right directed to the EU Parliament

We haven't missed the fact that the EU Parliament has contrived up a new controlling instrument in the framework of the discussion about the potential non-eligibility of certain initiatives, so-called constitutional initiatives – and sees itself here as controller. This type of function for Parliament would undermine the division of power anchored in the Lisbon Treaty which guarantees the citizens an equal access in regards to the initiative right.

Competition may generally energize commerce, but in constitutional questions, care must to be taken concerning type cleanness and a mesh of petition and initiative rights must thus be categorically rejected. An additional fact is that at EU level in contrast to Member States, several organs are appointed for legislation – although it is up to the Commission in the end to launch a formal legal initiative.

That is why the two initial tracts of citizens make thorough sense: with the petition right, the citizen directs him or herself to the EU Parliament, with the initiative right, to the EU Commission. This creates the prerequisites for a system which is mutually active. Nothing hinders EU initiative committees namely from increasing awareness in Parliament for its concern along the petition right; in this case one would actually have arrived at a positive, substantial, political competition and then the institutions could show how much they competitively care about citizen concerns.

Subsidies, Sponsorships, Counseling Assistance, Start-Up Aid

The "Ten Questions"

As already mentioned, a functional, trustworthy and a European Citizens' Initiative right which motivates the commitment of the citizens requires not only a regulatory but far more a supportive procedure legislation. This has, however, received almost no attention until now from the Commission. It is, in our opinion, perhaps the greatest omission of the Commission up to the present! We are hopeful that, with arguments, we will be able to convince the Commission to become correctively active here in the interest of democracy and Europe.

European Citizens' Initiatives are not to become an unordered extra-parliamentarian opposition of a few powerful opponents for lack of a systemic and systematic embedding: in that case, much power and a great promise for the positive formation of Europe would be senselessly lost.

Thus we draw attention here in broad strokes (and later in detail by addressing the single questions of the Green Paper) to the significance and elements of a supportive ECI infrastructure:

When someone – like the Commission and we, the European Citizens' Initiative Office, suggests doing without the formal eligibility examination process, it still does not unbind him or her from being of service to potential initiators with a consulting agency in an early stage of the considerations.

This can take place initially in the form of an online HelpDesk. In a second step, it will be important to advise EU initiatives in a direct and decentralized way and pose the "first ten questions" to them on the success or failure of an initiative. At this point in a ECI process, every question should be raised which would otherwise be examined in an eligibility examination procedure, like compatibility with human rights, the central Union values as well as the unity of the matter, the clarity of the formulation and naturally, whether the cited initiative concern falls within the competence of the EU Commission.

Initiative committees which go through this type of counseling might be given a kind of "Green Card" which would give the European people a signal regarding the eligibility of an initiative without the Commission itself or a Court having to enter the game.

In view of the proposed timeframe limitations for the collecting phase of signatures – between 12 and 18 months – the pre-collecting phase will take on decisive importance for the success of a concern. Besides the potential completion of the quantitative requirements, the reason for this is found in the qualitative facilitating of a pan-European dialog on a particular pertinent question.

Initiative committees will thus need to invest strongly in the preparation of a transnational support network in the run-up to an initiative launching process and should thus be advised specifically by this time. In addition the ECI online platform which the EU Commission has envisaged should offer services but also those in the beginning phase of independent, non-governmental agencies-run support agency like, for example, our "European Citizens' Initiative Office" (ECIO),

It would be feasible in this type of pre-procedure to recognize possible overlapping at an early stage and avoid unnecessary competitive initiatives. If it brings about parallel initiatives and duplication regardless, then this may not be allowed to become a hindrance. It is just as undesirable that an authority – as is the case in California – might be allowed to decide on the formulating of an initiative. Since it will depend on the EU Commission in the end how it deals with a successful initiative proposal, it is important that the greatest scope of freedom is ensured for the preparation and implementation of a European Citizens' Initiative.

IV. Questions and Answers - concerning the Green Paper questions in detail

1. The requirement of initiative vote spread across a "significant number of Member States".

Many numbers have been dealt with since the announcement of this requirement. Even a minimum of four states was argued to be sufficiently representational and systemic. For instance, as in the first report draft of the EU Parliament (prepared by Sylvia Yvonne Kaufmann), where it was thought that according to Art 76 TFEU, orientation to an interest in a European commonweal can already be implied with declarations by a fourth of the States. According to Art 76 TFEU, the right to submit a legislative proposal is given to a quarter of Member States – meaning 6 States. Thus the Parliament report draft concludes, an instrument which at its core is clearly only a summons to the Commission to submit a legislative proposal, may address an even lower quorum without contradiction – thus four.

Of course, a well-meaning low-lying number may possibly serve the legality determination but it will not be helpful for the political acknowledgement of legitimacy. Just think: individuals reach an agreement faster regionally than in a pan-European context. One example: an east-Mediterranean consensus which mobilizes a million people from Cyprus, Bulgaria, Greece and Malta or one from north-European with Latvia, Estonia, Lithuania and Finland would already meet the 4 State criteria.

Regardless of the preferential treatment of the European Citizens' Initiative Right we desire, a measurement set too low would be contraproductive. Since in this way, expectations would be nourished which could not then be met. The less an initiative is spread across Europe and as a result, only able to claim with difficulty that it is a reflection of a pan-European citizens' concern, the less the initiative may expect to have its concern taken seriously by the Commission.

Those who urge real assistance in favor of a prosperous European initiative form must take it when it comes from the other direction: we thus support the opinion of the Commission in the Green Paper regarding the thoughts on representation and with it, the recommended minimum number of nine qualified (cf. 2) Member States. This type of – admittedly – ambitious hurdle also makes it necessary simultaneously that the Commission also creates and provides pro-active support mechanisms.

2. Minimum Number of Signatories per Member State

We state first of all that we would also consider the requirement of 1 million as insufficient for a legitimate, as in popular vote-triggering, Citizens' Initiative right. Many States require considerably higher access percent number for good reasons. Thus in the EU constitutional convent discussions, at first higher qualification limits were named as well which were however then reduced to a million signatures in light of the mere agenda-setting and minimally binding character of the new instrument.

The Parliamentary report draft insufficiently interprets the representational criteria in our opinion if already a five-hundredth of citizens or, as the case may be, a four-hundredth of eligible voters is considered representative. We register herewith our doubt.

One should treat this new instrument not preferentially but as correctly as possible. It is what it is. And a million is still a million in a democracy based on counts. We don't discard barring clauses for the smallest of parties in parliamentary elections because in the meantime a few well-meaning folk could have joined together. It doesn't only have to do with finding out more about how the general public in Europe thinks but about how numerically important a political idea is or how a method of resolution stands compared to others. The finding and creating of political majorities, whether relative or absolute, belongs to the core business of democracy. The new European Citizens' Initiative right must be clearly differentiated not only from the petition right directed to the EU Parliament but also from the efforts of opinion surveys of opinion institutes and their momentary opinion polls.

The meeting of minimum conditions alone does not in our eyes create a positive point of departure. It would not be hard for the EU Commission in this case to counter the initiative that in this case 99.75% of European citizens do not share the concern of the initiative submitted – or even explicitly oppose it.

As part of the rebuttal of this type of argumentation, we suggest the following. It should be possible within the framework of the signature collecting to speak not only in favor of the initiative concern but also against. For this, however, it would have to be ensured that such negative signatures are not counted against it. Should the threshold of a million signatures in favor of the concern be reached (plus the required number of qualified Member States), then the initiative is achieved. The advantage of this type of option, with counter-signatures, is to be found in the resulting clearly expressed opinion of EU citizens. The EU Commission could use this as an important source for its political estimate of the further procedure. Once again it needs to be pointed out namely in this connection that the European Citizens' Initiative Right has to do on the one hand with an exclusively agenda-setting initiative right which, on the other hand, disposes of an indirect functionality as part of the EU-specific political system. In the end, it is the Commission itself which is responsible in instituting a formal initiative procedure.

Further, we consider the criteria of connecting Member States in Art 11.4 TEU from a primarily legal perspective as problematic if not false. This is because with European initiative right, we are dealing with a completely new instrument of a pan-European kind which does not have national citizenship as its basis but the Union citizenship. A membership state-like view of things is in fact unwanted in the case of the European Citizens' Initiative, since it, like the corresponding right of European Parliament and the European Council, deals with transnational, European initiatives. Logically that is why it is sensible to make the point of contact the address or the particular residence. Consequently, other criteria could qualify for the establishment of a representative spread, for instance, a representative spread across municipalities or regions.

We admit, however, that upon legal-organizational grounds, the determination of representation by way of the States would be the organizationally simplest means. Then, however, those with the right of residence, not State citizens but EU Parliament election-eligible EU citizens are counted within the quorum of place of residence and not the State of their formal national citizenship.

We agree with the Commission in the appraisal made in the GP that a state-related minimum of signature number per State would be the most unsuitable means. At the same time, however, a fixed key of one-five-hundredth as sole criteria is not especially suitable since it does not do the preliminary work for the principle of a pan-European representation which we are aspiring to. To the contrary, the implementation right should not leave any measure untried which encourages participation with the broadest and widest spread across the Union.

As was already described in the initial section of this article, that is why the introduction of a flexible system, a sliding scale system, is to be the goal with view to the widest participation and spread throughout Europe. In this, the minimum provenance of signatures which as the Commission suggests can come from a third of Member States (each with at least 0.2% of the total population) may serve as a point of departure, whereby as presented above, the country of residence is to be applied. Due to exactly this fundamental idea of a European spread with the broadest and at best, fullest coverage, compensation should be made possible of a failed minimum in one of the States with voting in several other States as the third of the States minimum. Whether one could demand a higher total number than the million signatures in this case via the implementation right seems doubtful upon legal grounds. That is why we suggest that those signatures which come from States which exceed the minimum number of eight States should compensate to offset the requisite of meeting the 0.2% key.

Let us bring to mind the requirements once again of the framework right of Art 11.4 TEU. Here, the number of 1 million is chosen as a minimum fixed size and the requirement of spread from a significant number of States as the variable size. By conclusion, the implementation right must strictly persevere to meeting the attainment of the one million signatures but is free in the arranging of variable components. Simultaneously, however, the "implementation regulator" is obliged to avoid new hurdles.
There is thus no legal hindrance for our suggestion of a sliding scale system.

3. Minimum Age

The wish would be for the broadest possible participation in initiatives. That is why the EU Parliament Report – allegedly preferentially – also suggests a minimum age of 16 years. The arguments here taken on their own are praiseworthy: Art 11.4 speaks of Union citizens without qualifying clauses like fundamentally mature, mature enough to vote or similar things which would point to a wide group of participants. In addition, a possible restriction of democratic participation should align itself to the proportionality principle which suggests non-exclusive positioning with an initiative right which is “weak” to begin with. And, finally, an age limit as low as possible is to be chosen – the report suggests 16 years – so that analysis contradictions could be avoided that could arise when in a State, Austria, the minimum age for the EP election was lower than participation set at an older age in a Citizens' Initiative.

We position ourselves thus along the lines of the suggestion made in the GP, which states regarding eligibility in an initiative that the voting right should be consulted, which is linked individually to the voting age of the National legal structures.

At the same time, it makes sense to amend this basic principle in the following way. Arising from the fundamental concept of Art 11.4 to provide the Commission with political impulses and summons for legislation by way of the initiative right, in order that the EU Commission for its part permits the will of the European citizen to flow into its law-making, there should also be the option for participation from those not (yet) eligible to vote – along the lines of a “shadow” signature collection. This type of signatures would of course not be decisive in determining the qualification. (As an virtual inspiration we refer to the initiative platform www.we-change-europe.eu) for testing and simulating these types of signature collection practices).

4. Form and Wording of a Citizens' Initiative

The constitutional text (Art. 11.4) knows only one single requirement which an initiative must respect – that there must be an appropriate competence with the Commission for the initiative concern.

In the GP, however, the Commission now suddenly brings several possible additional requirements to the discussion, although these, happily, are not to be given a great deal of weight from the Commission's point of view. Should however such additional limitations find inclusion in the ordinance draft of the Commission, then the ECJ will have to decide in the end on the constitutionality of it.

5. Requirements for the Collection, Verification and Authentication of Signatures

The fact that only the respective election offices (officially designated centers) come into question for the certification of submitted signatures is beyond discussion of any kind. The broad-sweeping comments in the GP in regards to the cooperation of Member States seem to us in this context to be a sensible statement of respect acknowledging the sovereign rights of Member States.

Further, we welcome the main statement: “to set a number of basic provisions at EU level and obligations for Member States to facilitate the collection process and remove unduly restrictive requirements.” In reality, there is namely cause to fear that the Member States might have tendencies to set additional hurdles in the way of their citizens at the European level – in particular within the context of how restrictive the discussion is held in some places today on the status of direct-democratic participatory rights in the representational system.

With this, two questions come into clear focus: how are signatures to be collected? And: what degree and scope is the control over these signatures to have?

Here we advise the EU Commission to adopt a relaxed and initiative-friendly attitude. Since, with the European Citizens' Initiative Right, we are dealing with a pan-European instrument and in addition, with a procedure which is aimed directly at the Commission. It is thus the Commission decision alone as to how welcoming it wishes to lean towards the citizenry legally, then it alone will have to bear the blows of possible criticism and dissatisfaction of citizens and media.

This is why the online initiative platform as planned by the GP is a central element to enable a citizen-friendly and effective initiative practice. This should facilitate the signature collection itself as well as the official management of the initiative (pre-process, registration, submission).

All other familiar forms are to be considered as well in the collection process itself like the traditional collection in the street (especially attractive in terms of discourse), the submission of signatures by mail and fax as well as the submission via a free-of-charge telephone hotline where "signatures" can be deposited. In the end, even the official registry office signature collection as is common with initiatives in some Member States needs to be checked. It makes sense to establish contact with the committees of the regions regarding whether the existing Europe Offices in the regions might not serve as an actual contact point.

About Verification and Authentication of Signatures

As has been presented in the preliminary fundamental section, we are dealing with the core of a (direct) democratic autonomy which is to be newly obtained of the Union versus the Member States.

Since it has to do with an instrument according to 11.4 TEU which is a genuine Union instrument, the EU Commission should insist that it alone decides what it deems sufficient in the authentication of the signatures it receives.

Since this is not a popular vote or election process with the European Citizens' Initiatives in which a few or even only one voice decides about agreeing on a factual issue or the voting down of a fraction, we think that a random sample process is sufficient. In this case, there are already global (very good) practices which contribute even more by ensuring that the bureaucratic effort is reduced.

The EU-wide common procedure regulations for the verification (certification) and authentication of signatures can also take the form that the

Commission directs arbitrarily-chosen "signature packets" for random sample control to Member States. Nothing more is needed. To the extent that there are a percentage of invalid signatures, then these are to be marked against an initiative in a key drawn up according to States.

In summary, the questions posed under point 5 can be answered as follows:

Signature collection should be made possible along all imaginable channels. In this respect, the kind of data of the signatory is to be provided which is necessary for the authentication which follows. The EU Commission must determine for each member country (or even sub-national jurisdiction) which information is required according to the particular vote register (registry for usages) so that a requested institution can undertake its task.

Security measures are to be taken which correspond to the requirements of data protection laws on the one hand and which promote the hindrance of forgery corresponding to the standard in the IT security market and according to the E-voting principles of the Council of Europe. Additionally the new form of e-collecting signatures in the framework of a legal right must create an innovative step-by-step process of introduction in order to safeguard the credibility of new democratic instrument.

The verification must comply with the law at place of residence because the participation in a signature collection is not the product of citizenship law but of Union citizen law.

Yes, there should be EU-wide common procedure rules because the instrument with which it deals is itself a Union instrument and thus there can only be one standardized verification procedure which is given to the authentication authorities. This is simply to be done in a way so that the designated authorities are able to conduct an efficient authentication according to their internal requirements.

There is to be, however, no latitude for specific precautionary measures by Member States except for the above-mentioned residual latitude stating that an authentication has to be in compliance with the national authentication requirements. This, however, is not presentational latitude.

Yes, the citizen should certainly have – along the lines even of first option – the possibilities of participating online. A pan-European initiative, with an objective glance at the literal requirements, will hardly be granted success without online methods. For this, online signatories must have the data at hand for those who need to be able to establish their voting legitimacy if subject to control. The protection of this data must correspond to the above-mentioned international principles and security standards. Should citizens not want to use this channel due to sensing lack of trust in data security with online signatures, then there must be other collection channels open to them. The question does not seem to us to be posed quite correctly also for another reason, since it will depend on the presentation of the implementation law as to how invitingly and with how many possibilities the EU will offer in the conducting of an initiative.

6. Time Limit for the Collection of Signatures

It is hardly helpful or expedient to draw on the time framework of Member State initiative laws as reference values. This is because in spite of the desirable homogeny of initiative requirements, there is still a list of additional barriers to be overcome, like first of all, language barriers or cultural disparities.

The grounds for setting of a time frame are chosen rightly. The suggested time limit of one year is chosen wrongly – particularly in the case where the Commission might not be willing to provide any additional support mechanisms in the context of something like a European Citizens' Initiative agency.

However, this time limit could be justified after all should the EU make use of our suggestions below:

One should think of having a pre-collection phase in which potential initiators can "simulate" the overall process and in this way already use the online tool provided by the Union – without however having to determine an official launching date for the initiative.

This procedure would offer several considerable advantages. European initiatives could already collect signatures with all the required information so that the signatories would participate later once again. Additionally, the EU Commission would have the opportunity to bring up its opinion informally regarding this initiative and should there be any cause for it, reduce potential later frustration with repercussions for Union consciousness.

This kind of pre-initiative phase could also be used further to better estimate the qualifications of an initiative in terms of subsidy eligibility. This is why we suggest that an initiative be considered qualified and thus worthy of support when it can account for 50,000 signatories.

7. Registration of Proposed Initiatives

We note with concern that suddenly, behind this innocuous title, the talk is of a kind of admission examination, which the Commission itself also described plausibly as undesirable.

An admission examination is to be refused because of grounds named earlier because this deeply interferes with the fundamental right endowment to freedom of expression. It is up to the EU Commission anyway, once the criteria are met, to state its position on how it intends to handle the demands of an initiative – by handing out a "green" or a "yellow" card. The political uproar will not be any less because the EU Commission reaches its decision already at an early stage by way of an admission examination. To the contrary, the EU Commission will only earn the accusation of "being judge and judged" and it would then in any case have to make its inadmissibility verdict compliant and pave the way to the ECJ.

Whether the issue and the instrument are better served by this is subject to doubt. No one can hinder the EU Commission from informing an initiative in the earliest phase that its concern will not be taken up on those grounds which must be used for the declaration of ineligibility. Thus, it would only create a hurdle which could upon some circumstances be overrun with help from the ECJ via a formal ineligibility declaration law which feeds the fundamental doubt that the EU Commission is negatively positioned to the instrument and thus itself constructs this kind of outlet in order to throttle an unwanted initiative. It would too quickly be possible to bring down constitutional, in particular, constitutional-amending initiatives with a statement of ineligibility. It should merely be clarified that EU Citizens' Initiatives cannot overrule the constitutionally guaranteed rights of Member States and as a consequence neither can it be expected by the EU Commission that it can.

It must suffice that the EU Commission may plead its own non-competence for a substantive issue at any point in time, even the earliest; initiatives should however remain at liberty to conduct their initiative on grounds of the basic provisions with freedom of opinion and freedom of expression. In the case of an initial "yellow" card, the EU Commission could refuse to give the support which we demand to an initiative which it has already informed that it considers its proposal to violate human rights or as contrary to the basic values in the TEU. However, it should be possible here on grounds of constitutional legality to claim the means of appealing to the ECJ.

When the EU Commission, which is discernable, thinks of an initiative which makes demands on the Commission which cannot be fulfilled, then the Commission can, after completion of an initiative always fall back on a series of tried and true objection figures for acute cases – like illegality or legal impossibility.

8. Requirements for Organizers – Transparency and Funding

The implication at outset is absolutely right: European Citizens' Initiatives cannot be conducted without support. We refer to American legal history. The introduction of a public subsidy scheme is now being vehemently demanded there precisely because of the proven susceptibility of citizen referendums, to only be able to take off with outside help and because of the inherent dangers of concealed lobbying using citizen initiatives.

It is astonishing that in the GP, the EU Commission however offers exactly opposite arguments and quite paradoxically. It states in the GP that is does not foresee any public subsidy "in the interest of preserving the independence and citizen-driven nature of initiatives." How is it then that public subsidy is the standard in national and regional contexts, in parliamentary as well as extra-parliamentary channels? It is just the opposite reasoning: in order that Citizens' Initiatives do not have to submit themselves to necessary private financing of unknown origin, or, as the case may be, essential initiatives which are not allowed to come into existence because it is lacking.

Because the disclosure of private support for private initiative organizers cannot be insisted upon by any legal guidelines of Union law whatsoever. According to individual national state laws, this kind of allocation falls under the classical civil law purview to which the Union has no right of access. An analogy to the disclosures along considerations of party funding law does not fit either. Since only through the bestowal of a subsidy provided with EU funds would a contractually-determined disclosure obligation be supported by contract law.

The EU Commission loses itself in this point in the same argumentation labyrinth in which the EU Parliament already lost itself. It is the EU Commission which must bear the accusation by the EU that it was not yet able or willing to introduce a strict transparency principle for its own activity in order to disclose the influences which are or were tried out on commissioners by lobbyists. And yet the Commission wishes with this starting position to burden down pro-active citizens with obligations which it itself has successfully avoided so far? This will certainly lead to stormy debates among public opinion which will be picked up gladly by the media and prove to be inclement for the starting climate of the European initiative law.

We recommend thus at this point thoroughly reconsidering the position of non-subsidy.

In achieving a subsidy scheme, we consider the counter call for maximum disclosure to be legitimate. Only by fulfilling this requirement do we affirm the question about disclosure – and we also consider it lawful and enforceable only then if at all.

The sober reminder that organizers "should" comply with the data protection requirements along national law we consider to be rhetorical idling. They have to, anyway. And by the way, it has become tradition that the person who wants to be trustworthy will offer a data protection policy far more extensive than the requirements of the data protection laws and will additionally submit to scrutiny laws and additional certification requirements. By the way, it will be up to the context of the nature of fundamental commerce as to whether private persons will be proffered sensitive data. The EU Commission should by the way not overlook the fact that we stand at a societal crossroads in which more and more people practically beg for as many options of self-disclosure as possible. It should thus be envisaged that supporters and promoters who wish self-disclosure can present themselves with the available Online Tool. A self-disclosure of this kind should be welcome in light of the desired transparency principle.

As a summary: freedom, in this case, freedom of expression may not be freedom for those who are privileged or substantiated from outside and supported from outside. It must be made possible for normal citizens to organize a pressing concern and negotiate a broad acceptance for their concern. That cannot be done without the pro-active help of the political community in whose context the initiative is undertaken (the provision of vouchers for online institutions, trips, meetings, publishing of printed material and much more). It should be the Union's intention to undertake everything so that initiatives can step forward with the highest qualification. The EU Commission must have the earnestness of the initiatives which it will be presented as its intention.

9. Examination of Citizens' Initiatives by the Commission

A remark which can very much be welcomed is the one on how and whether the Commission should react to a successful initiative in a specific time frame.

First of all, we recall that we are among those who consider the obligation to react to be one of the elements which belongs to political responsibility. Thus the EU Commission could bind itself to this kind of obligation to react or even in limited form only in a kind of law of self-obligation. That must remain up to the EU Commission's deliberation as to what it finds politically advantageous.

From the approach we have of not being so much concerned about individual initiatives as much as for a switching of paradigms in the European Union's political communication along the tracks of direct democracy, we would recommend to the EU Commission – self-obligatorily hasty at best – to abandon speed in favor of effective communication. (The GP causes confusion with the chosen formulating of sub 9, saying that proposed term period in the best case could begin with "the formal submission of the initiative". The formal submission is foreseen before, at the start of the time limit for the beginning of an initiative. It can thus only be meant after completion of this deadline, however that is determined – 12 months?)

If an initiative is to have 12 months time, which we think, as already stated, is much too short if one does not make a pre-preparation phase possible in a legal structure, then not much would speak against giving the Commission the same time limit. The Commission should definitely take time first to carefully consider the consequences and then arrive at a politically reasonable procedure which is of course would be put to vote by the States, their parliaments, the Council and the EU Parliament. Only then should it enter into a formal reaction procedure and only then make known its own possible initiative readiness.

10. Initiatives on One and the Same Issue

As already explained several times, the EU Commission should create advisory and supportive institutions and in undergirding them, though not politically, locate them in its near vicinity. This type of support structure would be created by a preliminary phase during which time information about initiatives, and also those which may be started parallel or even simultaneously, could become transparent.

However, at this point in the GP, the idea suddenly surfaces that a duplication or repeat of an initiative might "create undue burdens for the system" – and that thus an access limitation should be considered. Of which system? The idea of a system for promoting was (illogically) discarded in the GP until now. An online initiative platform can tolerate almost any kind of burden. The burden of a control system, which as we suggest is content with a statement-relevant sample, is within limits. So, once again, which system might be unnecessarily burdened? Instead, the mentioned point makes the purpose of what we suggest with an "early phase advisory system" much clearer which is conceived for taking up just these kinds of coordination tasks.

That is why there is full agreement when the EU Commission counters itself by stating that apparently identical themes might not be identical at all. The blocking of a subject with an initiative topic that was once submitted could even lead to highly undesirable processes. For instance, that a topic is seized in order to hinder that other initiators present it as well – and then perhaps not conducting it after all.

We can only caution discretion and recommend to the EU Commission that it respect European fundamental topics of freedom and citizen freedom.

Thus we caution urgently against any possible precautionary measures or hurdles.

V. Final Observations

We arrive thus in conclusion at the central question, which the GP has omitted, on how the purposeful use of the instrument of the European initiative with its identity-promoting, integrative, legitimation-fostering effects can truly be supported.

The one who really wants the initiative (in both senses) of the European citizens – this being the measurement of credibility of every responsible politician, and the EU Commission at the fore – needs to do something pro-actively for the initiative, needs to encourage, needs to enable, needs to promote, needs to also provide financial support, needs to equip initiatives. Many States have developed admirable models of support strategies already.

At the core, there are two premises:

The first deals with the function of numerical mightiness. Initiatives just barely at the limit of the minimum will only be able to develop a weak political significance and not be able to advertise themselves with it due to democratic-political correctness. Thus, should the concern of an initiative be considered incorrect in light of the Union, then the EU Commission should undertake everything to see that this need for clarification is carried out, in particular to also make the possible rejection by European citizens plausible to the initiators. Only in this way is it possible to retain political rationality when initiators themselves must acknowledge that their ambition in an honest and fair undertaking is not democratically viable in the form of an initiative.

The second premise has to do fundamentally with legitimacy. Legitimacy is linked not with the fastidiousness of the constitutional procedure as is often thought, but with what citizens experience, feel, think, sense, hope. When citizens complain in resounding unison that the Union is undemocratic or not democratically legitimized then this is a legal-political approach which must be counteracted with every possible strength available; thus the initiative law must be carried out as invitingly and generously as possible. It is not what is but how it is experienced which namely brings about or blocks legitimacy.

What was sorely lacking in the EU until now was the quietly implemented citizen conviction, a vague hope only, that in the unforeseen end, the EU might be accessible for the citizen. With Art 11.4, a spark of hope has been ignited which must be further fanned by the implementation law and by no means smothered. That is why the Commission should be very clearly advised to avoid any and everything which could be interpreted as secret reversals of the promises in the constitution. Not faintheartedness as to whether this instrument might become an additional problem factor: what's called for now is European courage!

Salzburg, January 31, 2010

Written and edited by the executive board of the European Citizens' Initiative Office

Johannes W. Pichler, Bruno Kaufmann, Andreas Gross, Anne-Marie Sigmund